MONEY BIBLICALLY
A Practical Guide to Financial Stewardship and Wealth-Building
Yeshua S. Jehu

Yeshua S. Jehu

Original concepts

This book presents original concepts and interpretations by Yeshua S. Jehu, offering a strong, insightful contribution to personal financial education. It fills critical gaps often overlooked, advancing financial literacy through a faithful approach that links practical knowledge with godly stewardship—an eye-opening perspective for those silently suffering from financial fragility. Designed as a practical tool for self-assessment and realignment, it equips readers to build lasting wealth with wisdom and purpose.

Bible Quotations:

Appreciation

To God Almighty, who in His infinite grace has granted me divine revelations, timely resources, strengthening counsel, and unwavering guidance through every season. I give profound thanks for His abundant wisdom, faithfulness, and sovereign hand that has sustained, inspired, and carried this work from inception to completion. All glory belongs to Him alone.

Contents

VISION FOR THE BOOK

"*There was a small town with only a few people, and a great king came with his army and besieged it. A poor, wise man knew how to save the town, and so it was rescued. But afterward no one thought to thank him. So even though wisdom is better than strength, those who are wise will be despised if they are poor. What they say will not be appreciated for long.*"
— Ecclesiastes 9:14–16 (NLT)

Likewise, if the church—armed with the wisdom of God by His Spirit and Word—does not secure a firm grip on this key pillar of human society, it will lose influence over entire communities. This has already been our story for generations. Though once revered for its power and witness, the church shrank back as the world advanced in wealth, deceived into calling poverty *piety*—a lie of the adversary designed to rob us of economic dominion and holy influence.

"Make it your goal to live a quiet life, minding your own business and working with your hands, just as we instructed you before. Then people who

are not believers will respect the way you live, and you will not need to depend on others." — 1 Thessalonians 4:11–12 (NLT)

The Church of God must be honorable and respectable in every way, giving the world no reason to perceive it as weak or lacking. Christian living extends beyond loving fellow believers; it demands responsibility in all areas of life. The world must see strength, integrity, and stature—even in physical and financial matters—before some can be won. Since finances is one of the three pillars that uphold society *(alongside sexuality and spirituality)*, the church's stewardship of this pillar directly influences how the world sees Christ's body. A positive image matters—standing in sufficiency, not in lack; in stewardship, not dependency; in noble abundance, not neediness that invites mockery rather than influence.

Yet this image must not be one of pride or the love of money, for many have corrupted the church's witness through extremes. Balance must return. Stewardship must be restored. That is the vision for this book: not merely to instruct, but to pair doctrine with practicality—priestly insight that equips you to govern wealth with purity, integrity, and spiritual strength. In this maturity, you wield wealth without being wounded by it. Therefore, whatever you do henceforth, do it faithfully, becoming a positive force in society and a light in the kingdom.

"...This is the church of the living God, which is the pillar and foundation of the truth." — *1* Timothy 3:15 (NLT)

It is the church's mandate to restore truth concerning the place of wealth as a pillar of human society—to handle it with maturity, free from corruption, so the love of money never consumes the believer but instead advances the interests of our Holy God.

And when wealth is righteously wielded, believers themselves become a blessing within the body. In Philemon—Paul's letter to a wealthy Greek landowner who hosted the Colossian church—Paul commended him for his faith, love, generosity, and the refreshing he brought to God's people. His wealth strengthened the church. His resources hosted the assembly. His stature empowered his ministry. *(Philemon 1:4-7)*

This is the pattern: *your wealth makes you a blessing in the work of God.* The advancement, the strengthening, the accommodation of God's work on the earth requires believers who wield wealth with purity and purpose.

PREFACE

"People ruin their lives by their own foolishness, and then are angry at the LORD."— *Proverbs 19:3 (NLT)*

The Church was never called to be poor—yet she has walked in poverty. She was designed for dominion—yet she has often surrendered that dominion through ignorance and mismanagement. Where the world mastered systems of increase, the Church romanticized scarcity as sanctity. Many have clothed mediocrity with the garment of humility and called it holiness. Others have mistaken lack for consecration, believing that to be poor is to be pure. Thus, the household of faith has suffered lack, not because God denied abundance, but because man distorted understanding.

This false doctrine—this perversion of divine economy—has taught generations to despise what Heaven designed to empower them. Yet Scripture is clear: *"If anyone regards something as unclean, then for him, it is unclean"* (Romans 14:14, NIV). When you label wealth as unholy, it becomes unholy to you. When you fear riches, you repel divine provision. It is not money that corrupts—it is the love of it (1 Timothy 6:10). Wealth in itself is a neutral servant, but a dangerous master.

Wealth, therefore, is not carnal—it is covenantal. It is an inheritance, a right, and a responsibility. The LORD declared, *"You shall lend to many nations, but you shall not borrow"* (Deuteronomy 15:6, NKJV). *"The blessing of the LORD makes one rich, and He adds no sorrow with it"* (Proverbs 10:22, NKJV). To live in lack is not proof of piety; it is evidence of misalignment. For the kingdom of God is not glorified when His ambassadors are beggars on the fields they were sent to rule.

Living to merely satisfy needs is not prosperity—it is captivity. For the poor live in the constant cycle of chasing after money, yet their needs remain unfulfilled. It is wealth that truly conquers needs—because wealth creates sustained provision, continuous flow, and freedom from the bondage of want. The poor chase money; the wise build wealth.

Wealth breaks the cycle of scarcity and establishes the believer in the covenant of abundance. *"The poor man is hated even by his own neighbor, but the rich has many friends"* (Proverbs 14:20, NKJV). *"The rich rules over the poor, and the borrower is servant to the lender"* (Proverbs 22:7, NKJV). Poverty strips a man of influence, while wealth amplifies his voice. Without it, the Church forfeits the ability to establish dominion in territories of governance, innovation, and culture.

Yet within the sanctuary, wrong voices have risen—teachers who glorify lack and vilify stewardship. They call greed what is actually diligence. They brand ambition as pride, and faith for provision as carnality. The Apostle warned, *"They must be silenced... they have already turned whole families away from the truth. Such teachers only want your money"* (Titus 1:11 NLT). These are the blind guides of the age, offering spiritualized excuses for their financial failures.

And so, the Church has wasted away beneath the weight of false teachings that paint wealth-building in the wrong light. Those who dare to teach it often do so only in fragments—speaking of the spiritual without teaching the practical. They tell men to "believe for wealth," but never show them how to build it. They emphasize faith but neglect financial intelligence. Yet the LORD never separated the two. Jesus Christ Himself spoke often about money management, stewardship, and accountability—more than He did about prayer or Heaven. Why then does the Church avoid what the Master made plain?

It is inadmissible to separate the spiritual from the practical, for the spirit is the spine of the structure. Money Biblically solves this imbalance. It restores divine symmetry—balancing the priestly and the practical, the spiritual and the systematic.

Each law and lesson within these pages merges both realms: the heavenly revelation and the earthly application. The believer must understand not only why God desires wealth for His people, but how to steward, multiply, and deploy it effectively. For without practical mastery, revelation remains theory; and without revelation, practicality becomes idolatry.

Beloved, wealth is not evil. The heart of man is deceitful; money merely magnifies what it finds there. Wealth is a gift—a tool in the hands of the righteous for the advancement of divine mandate. It is the power to establish God's covenant on earth *(Deuteronomy 8:18)*. But building wealth requires intention, discipline, and understanding. It is laborious work, but holy work. For by it, purpose finds the resources it needs to manifest.

Do not listen to those who mock abundance—they mock what they secretly desire but never attained. The blessing of the LORD adds no sorrow because it is divinely sustained. The wealthy of the world worry over their riches; their wealth rules them. But the believer's wealth is ruled by God. It is anchored in covenant, not in the fluctuations of market winds.

This book, *Money Biblically*, will unveil the practical wisdom and divine laws of money management according to Scripture. It will open your eyes to God's financial systems—how to build wealth faster and stronger, even within the brevity of time. You will also learn how the Church must handle money: how to steward it, multiply it, and deploy it for kingdom influence. For the lack of divine order in financial matters has caused much loss in the house of God. But this must no longer be so.

Most importantly, you will learn how to do it God's way. "Beloved, I pray that you may prosper in all things and be in health, just as your soul prospers."— 3 John 1:2

In the Greek, the word *prosper* means *"to have a good journey."* True prosperity, then, is to have a 'good trip' through this life—fulfilling divine purpose with sufficiency and peace. We are pilgrims on holy assignment, strangers on earth with Heaven as our destination *(Hebrews 11:13–16)*. To prosper, therefore, is to have everything necessary for a fruitful journey through time toward eternity.

Prosperity is not vanity—it is utility. It empowers the believer to execute divine purpose effectively. Money is not the purpose; it is the provision for purpose. And our stewardship over financial things is God's measure for entrusting us with true riches *(Luke 16:10–12)*.

So then, the message of *Money Biblically* is not about greed, but about grace. It is not about accumulation, but administration. It is not about vanity, but victory—the believer's ability to live in abundance, free from the bondage of need, and full of the capacity to bless others.

For it is written: *"Now He who supplies seed to the sower and bread for food will also supply and increase your store of seed and enlarge the harvest of your righteousness. You will be made rich in every way so that you can be generous on every occasion."*— 2 Corinthians 9:10–11 (NIV)

This is the covenant pattern of wealth—seed, increase, harvest, generosity. The more you sow, the more you grow. And in this increase, God is glorified.

Wealth, therefore, is not the goal. God is. But wealth is the means by which His will is established—both in your life and in His Church.

That is *Money Biblically.*

CHRIST'S loyal vassal,

JEHU :')

LESSON 1: THE SECRET TO FINANCIAL SUCCESS: WEALTH BUILDING ESSENTIALS

J UDGEMENT

The secret to financial success rests upon three pillars: spending, saving, and investing. These three—when set in order and held in right proportion—become the framework through which wealth multiplies, securing not only your future but your dominion in it.

It is written: *"Now He who supplies seed to the sower and bread for food will also supply and increase your store of seed and enlarge the harvest of your righteousness."*— 2 Corinthians 9:10, NIV

We are entrusted with three allocations:

- **Seed for sowing** — the future.

- **Bread for food** — the present.

- **Increase through compounding** — the multiplication of our seed over time.

The greater the increase, the greater the wealth. These three must remain in covenant rhythm—each feeding the other, none neglected.

The Formula of Financial Dominion:

1. Spend less than you make.

2. Save what you do not spend.

3. Invest what you save.

It all converges upon this: *Spending, Saving,* and *Investing.*

To succeed financially, you must master the sacred balance between the present and the future. If you spend excessively, you devour your seed. If you hoard excessively, you deny yourself the joy of your labor. The wise steward walks in proportionality—enjoying the fruit while preserving the seed.

Stored seed is destiny waiting. What is kept is not hoarded but prepared for increase. "Whoever sows generously will also reap generously" (2 Corinthians 9:6, NIV). This is a teaching on financial investment. God multiplies seed to enlarge your capacity to give and govern. Investment is divine foresight—compound interest is therefore, 'the compounding of your seed.' Thus, your store grows from surplus to abundance, from glory to glory, annually.

"And it is a good thing to receive wealth from God and the good health to enjoy it. To enjoy your work and accept your lot in life—that is indeed a gift from God."— Ecclesiastes 5:19 (NLT)

Balance, therefore, is the equilibrium where spending and saving coexist in rightful proportion. Yet note this: saving for the future weighs more heavily than spending for the present. It does not demand equal amounts, but correct proportions. For the man who saves rightly has already spent wisely.

To be financially out of balance is to live in quiet ruin. Overspend, and you rob your tomorrow. Undersave, and you enslave your future self. If you do not govern your finances, your finances will govern you.

(Illustration of balance in our context)

PRIESTLY APPLICATION

The ultimate result of increasing your seed is divine enrichment—not merely for personal comfort, but for kingdom capacity. You are made rich not to boast, but to bless; not to hoard, but to help.

"You will be made rich in every way so that you can be generous on every occasion, and through us your generosity will result in thanksgiving to God."—2 Corinthians 9:11, NIV

Wealth, therefore, is covenantal stewardship. As the world obsesses over methods to preserve their riches, the believer rests upon divine principles—knowing his increase is not luck, but law. God Himself enlarges the harvest, that each new cycle of sowing may exceed the former. Thus, the righteous become rich over time—not by haste, but by harmony with divine principle.

If you do not follow God's financial laws, you will remain subject to the world's financial curses. Prosperity is not an event—it is obedience in motion.

God's desire is not that we merely survive, but that we become channels of abundance—vessels through whom resources flow to accomplish His will. His perfect will is that you have sufficiency for yourself and surplus for others.

Therefore, discernment is required. Do not let the love of money blind you, nor let false humility rob you. Balance is paramount. The believer's relationship with money must be governed by revelation and restraint.

Money is not the mission—it is the means. It is the tool given for a good journey through this life (3 John 1:2), that the saint may walk in sufficiency, steward in wisdom, and serve in generosity.

LESSON 2: CHOOSING THE RIGHT CAREER: ACCEPTING YOUR LOT IN LIFE

JUDGEMENT

Choosing a career is not merely a practical choice—it is a divine alignment. For the believer, vocation is not just employment; it is deployment. It is the discovering of where Heaven has stationed you in the marketplace. Childhood impressions, parental examples, and societal pressures may shape your perception of work and wealth, but they must never define your destiny. The Spirit of Truth must interpret your life's calling—not culture, not comparison. When you discern your assignment through prayer, Scripture, and sober reflection, you find your portion under Heaven and peace accompanies your pursuit.

"Commit your works to the LORD, and your thoughts will be established"—Proverbs 16:3 (NKJV)

There is a global economic flood, and many are drowning for lack of wisdom. Yet in every crisis lies a turning point—one direction leading to ruin, the other to redemption. The power to determine which path you take lies in the financial and career choices you make today. Time, not talent, is the secret ingredient of wealth. And though the world may apply biblical principles and prosper—for *'the rain falls on the just and the unjust alike'* (Matthew 5:45)—only those anchored in divine prudence will sustain their increase without sorrow.

CAREER CHOICES: INFLUENCES AND BELIEFS

Our relationship with money is forged early—by observation, imitation, and expectation. *"Children's children are a crown to the aged, and parents are the pride of their children."* (Proverbs 17:6, NIV). The financial culture of your upbringing often becomes the template of your future. Yet you are not bound to repeat the patterns of the past. What was modeled may have molded you, but it cannot master you unless you submit to it. Relearn wealth through the Word. Break mental poverty with revelation. Govern your financial life through wisdom, not wounds.

This age markets vanity as value. The media equates self-worth with price tags and applause. Without discernment, many trade their seed for status—buying symbols instead of building substance. They splurge what should have been sown, chasing fleeting pleasures while forfeiting lasting prosperity. The cycle repeats until revelation intervenes. Recognize the pattern, and you will rise above it.

There are two mindsets: *scarcity* and *abundance*. Scarcity sees limits, abundance sees possibilities. The one hoards and loses; the other invests and multiplies. *"He who sows sparingly will also reap sparingly, and he who sows bountifully will reap bountifully"* (2 Corinthians 9:6, NKJV). Wealth is built not on fear, but on faith—on the courage to act when opportunity knocks.

THE MEDICINE OF CONTENTMENT

Be content with your lot in life. *"Better to have little, with fear for the LORD, than to have great treasure and turmoil"* (Proverbs 15:16, NLT). Your career is not random—it is your platform of dominion. Choose it prayerfully, not emotionally. It determines the rhythm of your provision, the reach of your influence, and the shape of your stewardship. Seek the counsel of the Spirit, not the crowd. Let your calling fit your divine design, and your work will flow from rest, not restlessness.

If you have already chosen a path, refine it. Ask God how it fits His greater blueprint for your life. Perhaps your current role is the bridge to your true assignment—do not despise it. Feed your spirit with the medicine of contentment, for discontentment corrodes destiny. Wealth without peace is poverty disguised.

PRIESTLY APPLICATION

Learn the holy art of contentment. *"For I have learned in whatever state I am, to be content"* (Philippians 4:11, NKJV). True wealth is not only earned—it is enjoyed. *"It is good for people to eat, drink, and enjoy their work... and to accept their lot in life. It is a gift from God"* (Ecclesiastes 5:18–19, NLT). Solomon teaches that prosperity without pleasure is futility—*'A stillborn child is better off than he who cannot enjoy his prosperity'* (Ecclesiastes 6:3).

Therefore, choose work that brings joy and fruit, where grace and diligence meet. Your career is your calling clothed in labor. Accept your lot, enjoy your work, and live in the quiet wealth of divine satisfaction—for it is God who gives both riches and the power to enjoy them.

LESSON 3: FINANCIAL LITERACY: UNDERSTANDING FINANCIAL CONCEPTS

J**UDGEMENT**

Money is not merely a means of survival; it is a divine instrument for stewardship and dominion. It is the tool through which opportunities are created, wealth is multiplied, and purpose is funded. The wise do not chase money—they master it. To do so, one must understand it. Financial literacy is the light that illuminates your path to stability and strength. Without understanding, wealth slips through the fingers like sand. But with wisdom, every coin becomes a seed, every decision a step toward increase.

"Be diligent to know the state of your flocks, and attend to your herds; for riches are not forever" (Proverbs 27:23–24, NKJV).

Scripture commands not ignorance, but oversight. You cannot manage what you do not monitor. Know where your resources are, where they go, and what they produce. That is the discipline of the wise steward.

Even among high earners, many live in quiet financial slavery—bound to debt, dependent on constant income, fearful of interruption. A single missed paycheck would dismantle their comfort. But the believer, armed with understanding and guided by prudence, breaks this cycle. Knowledge of money's principles frees you from uncertainty and positions you for abundance.

THE PILLARS OF PRUDENT FINANCIAL MANAGEMENT

True stewardship is not about reacting to financial storms but preparing before they come. It is about planning, managing, and multiplying with divine foresight. Wealth grows where wisdom governs. To manage your finances well is to master the art of alignment—ensuring every resource serves a purpose, every decision sows toward increase, and every opportunity is seized with discernment.

THE FOUNDATIONS OF YOUR FINANCIAL STEWARDSHIP

1. Personal Budget — Your Financial Game Plan

A budget is the foundation of financial order—the map of your money's mission. It is not bondage; it is strategy. It tells your money where to go before your emotions do. A budget is spiritual discipline in practical form—it reflects accountability, foresight, and mastery over impulse.

Purpose: A budget brings intention and control. It sets guardrails around your destiny, ensuring that each decision honors your future. It transforms chaos into clarity, protecting your wealth from leaks and your peace from anxiety. Freedom is not found in spending freely—it is found in spending wisely.

HOW TO BUILD YOUR BUDGET

Track every source of income and expense. Be brutally honest. List everything—salary, royalties, dividends, capital gains, side ventures.

Categorize expenses into fixed and variable. Fixed *(rent, utilities, insurance)* remain stable. Variable *(entertainment, dining, leisure)* fluctuate and reveal discipline.

Discern your patterns. Every purchase tells a story. Read it carefully to uncover leaks and habits.

Divide your spending into six key categories:

CATEGORY	NOTES (Prudent Financial Stewardship for a Believer)
Savings and Tithe	Non-negotiable. These are sacred allocations—the foundation of faithful stewardship.
Housing	Generally fixed; essential for stability but must fit within reason and order.
Transportation	Generally fixed; a necessity for mobility, but should serve, not strain.
Healthcare	Essential and often non-negotiable; guard your health as you guard your wealth. *(Ecclesiastes 5:19)*
Food	Essential nourishment; flexible but must remain disciplined.
Entertainment	Variable; your first 'sacrificial lamb' when cutting back.

The fixed categories form your foundation—never compromise them. Entertainment is fluid and the first to yield when adjustments are needed.

THE LIVING BUDGET

A budget is not carved in stone; it breathes with your life. As your seasons shift—career transitions, family growth, relocation—your budget must adapt. Regular review keeps you aligned with your financial goals and prevents drift.

This disciplined approach is the cornerstone of all financial wisdom. It ties your intention to your outcome and transforms stewardship into strategy. In the next lesson, we go deeper—into the art of building and managing your budget as a divine instrument for wealth, peace, and purpose. Adapt it to your specific situation.

"Through wisdom a house is built, and by understanding it is established; by knowledge the rooms are filled with all precious and pleasant riches" (Proverbs 24:3–4, NKJV).

2. Personal Income Statement — Knowing the State of Your Flocks

Once your budget—the blueprint of your financial plan—is in motion, the next step is to measure what truly transpired. This is where the Personal Income Statement becomes your compass. It records your real results—every stream of income, every expense, every decision made with your resources—and reveals whether you have governed your finances with prudence or drifted from your plan.

"Be diligent to know the state of your flocks, and attend to your herds; for riches are not forever" (Proverbs 27:23–24, NKJV). The income statement is that diligence in motion. It unveils the truth about your stewardship—what came in, what went out, and what remains.

Purpose: The income statement shows your actual financial performance by calculating your net result—income minus expenses. A positive margin is not just surplus; it is seed—capital for saving, investing, giving, and debt elimination. A negative result exposes leaks that must be sealed. Wisdom begins with awareness.

This report should be prepared at the close of each period—monthly, bimonthly, or quarterly. Regular review trains you to see patterns, measure growth, and make spirit-led adjustments. The wise do not guess their state—they know it.

<table>
<tr><td colspan="2" align="center">INCOME STATEMENT
As of Period: [Your Chosen Period]</td></tr>
<tr><td>INCOMES</td><td>Amount</td></tr>
<tr><td>Salary</td><td>[Amount]</td></tr>
<tr><td>Royalties</td><td>[Amount]</td></tr>
<tr><td>Investment Returns</td><td>[Amount]</td></tr>
<tr><td>Dividends</td><td>[Amount]</td></tr>
<tr><td>Capital Gains</td><td>[Amount]</td></tr>
<tr><td>Total Income</td><td>[Sum of All Incomes]</td></tr>
<tr><td>EXPENSES</td><td>Amount</td></tr>
<tr><td>Tithes and Savings</td><td>[Amount]</td></tr>
<tr><td>Housing</td><td>[Amount]</td></tr>
<tr><td>Healthcare</td><td>[Amount]</td></tr>
<tr><td>Food</td><td>[Amount]</td></tr>
<tr><td>Transportation</td><td>[Amount]</td></tr>
</table>

INCOME STATEMENT	
As of Period: [Your Chosen Period]	
INCOMES	**Amount**
Givings/Donations	[Amount]
Entertainment	[Amount]
Other Expenses	[Amount]
Total Expenses	**[Sum of All Expenses]**
| NET-INCOME CASH FLOW *(Margin)* **| = Total Income – Total Expenses |**	

Think of it as your personal profit and loss statement—a reflection of your ability to multiply what God has entrusted to you. Whether small or great, every steward must give account. The income statement becomes your accountability mirror before God and yourself.

Your *Net-Income Cash Flow*, or *Financial Margin*, is what remains after all obligations are met. This is your strength. From this margin, you secure your future—saving, investing, or giving strategically. Always treat tithes, givings, and savings as sacred allocations—non-negotiable commitments that anchor both your financial and spiritual security. They are not losses; they are sowings into divine multiplication.

In essence, your Personal Income Statement is a mirror of stewardship. It shows whether you are advancing toward wealth or drifting toward want. With each review, you sharpen foresight, discipline, and divine balance. It is written: "Through wisdom a house is built, and by understanding it is established" (Proverbs 24:3). So too, through understanding your finances, your future is secured.

3. Personal Balance Sheet: Knowing Your Net Worth

Now that your net income is clear, the next discipline is to prepare your balance sheet—a financial mirror that shows where you truly stand. It captures your position at a moment in time: what you own *(assets—cash, investments, property)* and what you owe *(liabilities—debts, loans, obligations)*. Your net worth is the difference.

Purpose: The balance sheet reveals your financial strength—your dominion in numbers. It is a snapshot of assets, liabilities, and equity as of a single date, exposing whether you stand in surplus or deficit. For true financial health, your assets must outweigh your liabilities. That is rightful order.

Classic Equation:

Assets = Liabilities + Equity

Personal Finance Equation:

Net Worth = Assets − Liabilities

Calculate this at least once a year—or as often as you review your finances—for these statements are interwoven, forming a complete picture of your stewardship.

CATEGORIZING YOUR ASSETS

List assets in order of liquidity—how quickly they can be converted to cash:

Current assets: Cash, checking accounts, emergency funds, and intangible assets that generate passive income.

Invested assets: Mutual funds, stocks, retirement savings accounts, long-term Guaranteed Investment Certificates (GICs) or Certificates of Deposit (CDs), and bonds.

Solid (hard) assets: Tangible holdings like income-producing real estate, gold, silver, commodities, machinery, and collectibles. These hedge against inflation and diversify your portfolio.

CATEGORIZING YOUR LIABILITIES

Current liabilities: Credit card balances, personal debts, maintenance, utilities, short-term bills.

Fixed liabilities: Rent, insurance, mortgages—predictable and recurring.

Long-term liabilities: Auto loans, extended mortgages, and multi-year debts.

Liabilities are cash-consuming obligations.

Maintain liquid assets greater than liabilities to preserve stability and freedom.

When total assets exceed liabilities, your foundation is solid. Continue to build, multiply, and fortify. If the reverse, let it serve as your starting line—focus your energy on increasing active income and reducing debt.

DORMANT ASSETS AND ACTIVE LIABILITIES (DA.ALs)

Not every asset works for you. Dominion demands discernment. Some assets, though valuable on paper, remain dormant—idle, producing no income—while still generating active liabilities that drain your resources. This is what I call the *"Dormant Asset-Active Liability"* dynamic.

A personal residence, though valuable, often generates no income yet carries taxes, mortgages, and upkeep. A personal vehicle holds resale value but demands fuel, insurance, and repairs. These *DA.ALs* subtly erode wealth as 'money pits' while giving an illusion of prosperity.

Why it matters: Wealth is not what you hold—it's what works for you. Recognizing *DA.ALs* breaks the illusion of wealth by possession and shifts focus to wealth by productivity.

ACTION STEPS:

Identify dormant assets and list them at the bottom of your balance sheet under assets.

Link their tied liabilities—mortgages, maintenance, or loans to the liabilities side of your balance sheet.

Convert or control: Monetize or minimize. Rent unused property, reduce dependency on draining assets, and redirect freed capital into income-generating ventures.

PERSONAL BALANCE SHEET	
As of [Date]	
ASSETS	**LIABILITIES**
Cash & Checking Accounts	Credit Cards
Emergency Fund	Personal Loans
Intangible/Passive Income Assets	Home & Vehicle Maintenance
Mutual Funds, Stocks, Retirement Accounts	Utilities
Long-term GICs/CDs, Bonds	Insurance Premiums
Real Estate (Income-Producing)	Mortgage/Rent
Precious Metals & Collectibles	Auto Loans
Primary Residence *(DA.AL)*	Other Long-term Loans
Automobiles *(DA.ALs)*	
Personal Property *(DA.AL)*	
Total Assets	**Total Liabilities**
Net Worth = Assets − Liabilities	

THE PATH TO TRUE WEALTH

Faithful stewardship is not in accumulation but activation. Ownership means little if what you own does not serve your dominion. Shift from hoarding to harnessing—from idle possession to active productivity.

This revelation grants clarity: you are not rich because of what you possess, but because of what your possessions produce. That is the power of divine stewardship—seeing beyond the numbers into the flow.

4. Cash Flow Statement

Now that your net worth is established, the next instrument of dominion is your cash flow statement—the pulse of your financial life. It draws from your income statement and balance sheet to reveal how cash truly moves: where it enters, where it exits, and what remains. Did your resources multiply, or did they diminish? This statement exposes your financial liquidity—the lifeblood of your stewardship.

Purpose: The cash flow statement unveils your capacity to generate, direct, and manage cash—determining whether your system is expanding or contracting. It reflects whether you are a faithful steward in motion or stagnant in flow.

Prepared last among the core statements, it captures all inflows and outflows across the period, emphasizing liquidity—not mere profitability.

CASH FLOW COMPONENTS

Inflows: All income streams—salary, business revenue, royalties, and investment gains.

Outflows:

Savings and Tithe – Non-negotiable. These are not expenses; they are covenants. They sanctify your income and fortify your foundation. Prioritize them first to guard against misdirection of seed.

Fixed Outflows – Obligatory payments such as mortgage/rent, car loans, insurance (auto, home, health), property taxes, and student loans. Predictable and consistent.

Variable Outflows – Flexible expenses like maintenance, food, entertainment, travel, clothing, and miscellaneous costs. These can be trimmed or expanded based on your financial season.

Wise control over variable expenses expands your financial margin, allowing overflow to reinvest, save, or reduce debt.

If your net cash flow is positive, you have governed your finances well—multiplying what was entrusted to you. If negative, it is not defeat but revelation—a mirror showing where to recalibrate, realign, and restore flow.

SIMPLE CASH FLOW STATEMENT	
Cash Flow Statement **As of [Date]**	
INFLOWS & OUTFLOWS	**AMOUNT**
INFLOWS	
Salary	[Amount]
Royalties	[Amount]
Investment Income	[Amount]
Other Income	[Amount]
Total Inflows	[Sum of Inflows]
OUTFLOWS	
Savings & Tithe	[Amount]
Total Savings & Tithe	[Sum]
Mortgage / Rent	[Amount]
Car Payments	[Amount]
Insurance (Auto, Home, Health)	[Amount]
Property Taxes	[Amount]
Student Loans	[Amount]
Total Fixed Outflows	**[Sum]**

SIMPLE CASH FLOW STATEMENT Cash Flow Statement As of [Date]	
INFLOWS & OUTFLOWS	**AMOUNT**
OUTFLOWS	
Home Maintenance	[Amount]
Food	[Amount]
Entertainment	[Amount]
Travel	[Amount]
Clothing	[Amount]
Miscellaneous	[Amount]
Total Variable Outflows	**[Sum]**
| NET CASH FLOW (Inflows − Outflows) | [Amount] |	

HOW THE FINANCIAL STATEMENTS INTERLOCK

Budget: The plan—where your money should go before it moves.

Income Statement: The record—what actually came and went.

Balance Sheet: The position—your assets, liabilities, and equity in time.

Cash Flow Statement: The motion—how liquidity moves through your system.

When these four operate in harmony, your finances speak one language—order. Positive net worth joined with positive cash flow births expansion. Negative figures, however, reveal weak gates—warning you to guard, correct, and restructure.

This cycle of planning, recording, positioning, and flowing builds mastery over money. It transforms stewardship into strategy, and strategy into dominion.

ESSENTIAL FINANCIAL CONCEPTS FOR PROSPERITY

Financial literacy is not worldly wisdom—it is priestly stewardship. It governs how believers handle what Heaven entrusts to their hands. Mastering these foundational principles positions you for dominion in the financial realm.

CREDIT SCORE — THE CURRENCY OF TRUST

Your credit score is not merely a number; it is a reflection of your financial character. It signals integrity, reliability, and discipline in managing what has been borrowed. In today's system, this score determines access—whether for housing, credit, or opportunity.

A standard credit score ranges between **300** and **850**, derived from five key factors:

1. Payment History (35%): Faithfulness in payment is the weightiest factor. Timely payments prove reliability; missed payments, defaults, or bankruptcies tarnish your record and trustworthiness.

2. Credit Utilization (30%): This measures how much of your available credit you use. Keeping utilization below 30% reflects control, restraint, and wisdom. The less you use, the stronger your testimony of discipline.

3. Length of Credit History (15%): Longevity reveals consistency. Older accounts demonstrate endurance and stable stewardship over time.

4. Types of Credit (10%): A healthy mix—credit cards, mortgages, installment loans—shows maturity in handling diverse financial responsibilities.

5. New Credit Inquiries (10%): Each application leaves a "hard inquiry." Too many inquiries signal desperation, not discretion. Guard your credit record as you would your reputation.

Improving Your Score: Be faithful in payments. Reduce debt deliberately. Keep utilization low. Review your report regularly, correcting any errors or fraudulent entries.

Why This Matters: A strong credit score can save you thousands in interest and unlock opportunities otherwise closed. It affects your loans, rent, insurance rates, and even employment prospects. For the wise, understanding credit is not optional—it is essential.

"A good name is to be chosen rather than great riches, and loving favor rather than silver and gold." — Proverbs 22:1 (NKJV)

COMPOUND INTEREST — THE MULTIPLICATION PRINCIPLE

Called the eighth wonder of the world, compound interest is Heaven's mirror in finance—it multiplies what you steward faithfully. It is the law of increase through consistency: interest earning upon interest, wealth compounding through time.

If you invest **$2,000** at **5%** annual interest, the first year earns **$100**, totaling **$2,100**. The next year, you earn **5%** on **$2,100**, not $2,000—yielding about **$105**. This continuous snowballing effect accelerates wealth creation.

Time is your greatest ally. The earlier you sow, the greater your harvest. The frequency of compounding—annual, semi-annual, quarterly, monthly, or daily—determines the speed of growth. The more frequent, the faster your wealth multiplies.

This principle applies beyond savings—into investments, stocks, and dividends. When you reinvest your returns, you harness the power of compounding. It is not just your money working—it is your money serving you continually.

"So he who had received five talents came and brought five other talents, saying, 'Lord, you delivered to me five talents; look, I have gained five more talents besides them.'. His lord said to him, 'Well done, good and faithful servant; you were faithful over a few things, I will make you ruler over many things.'" — Matthew 25:20-21 (NKJV)

PRIESTLY APPLICATION

Financial wisdom is not carnal strategy; it is divine order expressed through diligence, foresight, and understanding.

"To acquire wisdom is to love yourself; people who cherish understanding will prosper." — Proverbs 19:8 (NLT)

Wisdom multiplies wealth. Neglect destroys it. Commit to every project, never stop half-way.

"Lazy people take food in their hand but don't even lift it to their mouth." — Proverbs 19:24 (NLT)

Act swiftly. Steward deliberately. Delay is decay.

"The prudent understand where they are going, but fools deceive themselves." — Proverbs 14:8 (NLT)

A budget is your first step toward foresight. It translates intention into action.

"Work brings profit, but mere talk leads to poverty." — Proverbs 14:23 (NLT)

Commitment, accountability, and responsibility are the three pillars of financial faithfulness—guarding your promises, guiding your actions, and grounding your progress.

CAUTION: YOUR STANCE ON CREDIT MONEY

Credit is not income—it is borrowed trust. It is temporary, costly, and bound by obligation. As stewards of divine provision, we must resist the snare of living beyond our means. *"The borrower is servant to the lender."*

(Proverbs 22:7, NKJV) Debt may promise comfort, but it purchases captivity.

Credit itself is neutral—a tool, not a master. Used wisely, it builds credibility; used carelessly, it births bondage. The undisciplined live off credit because their storehouses are empty, forfeiting seed for survival. The wise, however, use credit only to strengthen standing, not sustain lifestyle—repaying balances in full, avoiding interest, and keeping dominion over debt.

Let discipline govern your spending. Build credit, but never depend on it. Spend from substance, not from speculation. Use credit as a tool for strategic credit score building, no more. True wealth flows from restraint and stewardship—sowing, saving, and ruling your resources with wisdom. Debt is not your portion; dominion is.

LESSON 4: BUDGETING FOR PROSPERITY: THE STEWARD'S GUARDRAIL

J UDGEMENT

Humility is a great safeguard against financial downfall. To live within your means is not weakness—it is wisdom. Many today drown in debt to maintain an illusion, chasing symbols of wealth that even the wealthy themselves can afford only because they mastered restraint. Do not imitate another man's fiction; establish your own reality. Even kings live within their means. True power is not in what you flaunt, but in what you sustain. A fool sacrifices substance for status; but the wise build silently, letting their stewardship speak. A budget is your guardrail—it keeps your chariot on the road of increase. Build it upon humility and prudence, and in due season, your wealth shall grow securely beneath your dominion.

"Some who are poor pretend to be rich; others who are rich pretend to be poor."
— Proverbs 13:7 (NLT)

BUDGETING

A budget is your financial covenant of order—a written decree over your income and expenses for a set time. It is the discipline that keeps you from the snare of financial ruin while propelling you toward divine increase.

In budgeting, balance is sacred. Needs are essential for survival, but life is to be enjoyed, not endured—thus wants are permitted, though always the first to be sacrificed when prudence demands. The world may use rules like the *50/30/20* rule; 50% to needs, 30% to wants, and 20% to savings or debt payment, but the believer's covenant adds another realm: tithe and generosity. These are non-negotiables—holy portions never to be touched.

Before a single coin is spent, determine your percentage demarcations—the boundaries of your financial structure. These categories bring order, restraint, and foresight.

PERCENTAGE DEMARCATIONS (FOR A SINGLE PERSON)

Tithe & Savings — 20%: Tithe (10%) belongs to God—the Principle of First-fruits. Savings (10%) belongs to you—pay yourself second. In time, this percentage can increase as you grow in mastery.

Housing — 35%: Includes rent or mortgage, utilities, property tax, insurance, and maintenance—everything required to possess and preserve your dwelling.

Transportation — 14%: Public transit fees, car payments, fuel, insurance, and maintenance—all that sustains your movement.

Healthcare — 13%: Insurance premiums, co-pays, prescriptions, and essentials for your physical body wellness.

Food — 12%: Both groceries and dining. All should fall within this parameter.

Entertainment — 6%: Recreation is allowed, but never rule-breaking. Joy is a companion, not a master.

EMERGENCY FUND

At the beginning, your savings also serve as your emergency fund. Once you've saved the equivalent of *three months' salary*, the recommended amount is *3-9 months*. You may transition portions of those funds toward investment after attaining the minimum goal. This process of saving will take roughly 2½ years—but remember, time is the currency of wealth. The earlier you begin, the greater your compound reward.

<u>*Consider a salary of **$4,337**:*</u>

SIMPLE BUDGET: SINGLE PERSON		
Category	Percentage	Amount
Tithe & Savings	20%	$867.40
Housing	35%	$1,518.00
Transportation	14%	$607.18
Healthcare	13%	$563.81
Food	12%	$520.44
Entertainment	6%	$260.22
Total	**100%**	**$4,337.00**

UNBREAKABLE RULES

-You cannot go **OVER** what is allotted for each category.-You must stay **UNDER** the amount allotted.

Your budget is your covenant of stewardship—break it, and you break your guardrail of increase. Savings is part of your no-touch category. The minimum is 10%; the recommended goal is 20%. You only increase it through margin birthed by prudence, not through emotion or impulse.

Never touch your savings. That is self-sabotage. To save is to pay yourself; to dip into your savings is to rob your own future. Your savings serve two divine purposes: as emergency protection and as seed for future investment.

"If anyone will not work, neither shall he eat." — 2 Thessalonians 3:10, NKJV

Revelation: If you lack the strength to produce, you lack the right to consume. To live beyond your means is to eat from what you have not yet earned—an act of financial rebellion. Stay within your measure.

He who produces has earned the right to partake; he who restrains preserves the power to increase. Discipline is the difference between stewardship and struggle.

FINANCIAL MARGIN

The more you stay under your allotment, the greater your margin—the space between what you could spend and what you actually spend. Margin is your wealth incubator. It cushions your future and feeds your investments.

If you overspend, you'll inevitably chip into your no-touch category—Savings and Tithe—the often *Victim of the Undisciplined*. That is why many never invest nor retire in peace.

When asked, "Where do things like clothing, school trips, pets, or haircuts fit?" — the answer is simple: those are luxuries funded by margin. Stay under each category; what remains becomes your discretionary joy.

Should any category bleed, let Entertainment be the first and only sacrifice. A simple budget trains your hands for war and your mind for restraint. Frugality is not sin—it is strategy. :')

THE STEWARD'S GUARDRAIL

A personal budget is not a prison; it is a pathway. It empowers informed spending and keeps your financial chariot on course. Through it, even your heavenly assignments dependent on resources find footing.

When your finances are structured in order, you have nothing to fear. Heaven defends those who honor divine principle.

"Moreover, it is required in stewards that one be found faithful." — 1 Corinthians 4:2, NKJV

TRACKING YOUR FINANCIAL ARK

Track your finances diligently. Update your statements often so you know whether you are growing or decaying. Technology has made this simple—use it. Many banks and apps now offer automated budgeting tools. Don't despise the advantage; it makes stewardship lighter and more efficient. Whether you track through an app, spreadsheet, or journal, consistency is the tool of accuracy.

Your records reveal the health of your financial ark—its leaks, its direction, its strength. Stay aware, stay watchful, stay wise.

THE IMP OF IMPULSE

Impulse buying is a thief in disguise—a tiny leak that sinks mighty ships. Small, frequent indulgences seem harmless, yet together they drain your flow like hidden termites.

Discipline shuts these doors. If an item isn't budgeted for or within your created margin, it is taboo.You may set aside a miscellaneous allowance later—but not before margin exists. Overindulgence is wrong; wise enjoyment is balance. Track. Cut. Reclaim. Your financial health will thank you.

"Catch us the foxes, the little foxes that spoil the vines." — Song of Solomon 2:15, NKJV

DORMANT ASSETS-ACTIVE LIABILITIES (DA. ALs)

Your house and car must match your means. Never buy symbols that strangle your liquidity. Living above your level invites money pits, not prosperity. When the economic floods come, pretenders drown first.

Live within your financial strength—neither strained nor cheap, but balanced. Adapt your lifestyle to fit your percentage demarcations. For students and starters, share costs, room together, or pool resources. These are not downgrades—they are temporary strategies for permanent elevation.

"Where no oxen are, the trough is clean; but much increase comes by the strength of an ox." — Proverbs 14:4, NKJV

Be willing to bear present inconvenience for future increase. The stable may be messy, but the ox builds abundance. :')

PRIESTLY APPLICATION

Seek the LORD while He may be found, that when the mighty waters rise, they will not find you unprepared. *(Isaiah 55:6; Psalm 32:6)*

By obeying His principles of stewardship, you invite His favor to rest on your financial house. When the storms come, your structure shall stand.

Pray over your finances continually. Prayer prevents emergencies; wisdom prepares for them. Both are divine.

Building an emergency fund is not unbelief—it is obedience. Faith does not negate planning; it perfects it. Your emergency fund is a tender shoot—guard it, grow it, and in time it shall shade you from life's unexpected heat.

LESSON 4 PART B: CREATING MORE MARGIN IN YOUR BUDGET

Creating margin in your finances must be an intentional pursuit each time income enters your system. As you steward it, your mind should immediately engage in ways to 'maximize your financial margin' while 'minimizing unnecessary expense.' Seek opportunities to save—adjust variable costs without compromising quality, embrace discounts, negotiate favorable interest rates, use reward points wisely. Every act of prudence enlarges your storehouse of seed—your savings for sowing, and your shield against uncertainty.

Understanding how you spend determines how you grow. Awareness births discipline; discipline births increase. By tracking every inflow and outflow, you gain clarity to set realistic goals—especially for your emergency fund. Think of it, and every other savings account, as your fortress of future security. Your emergency fund is your first line of defense when financial storms strike. This is not a lack of faith—it is the substance of it. *'Faith without works is dead.'* — James 2:17

Once your goal amount is set, start small. Small contributions, made consistently, compound into abundance. Apply automation—let technology serve you. Set automatic transfers from your chequing to your savings each time income arrives. It removes decision fatigue and enforces obedience.

Think of automation as your *financial servant,* faithfully executing your stewardship—alert, consistent, tireless.

When choosing where to store your savings, choose accounts that work while you rest. Apply the principle of compound interest—the silent builder of wealth. High-yield savings accounts and TFSAs *(Tax-Free Savings Accounts)* are wise choices; they allow your seed to grow tax-free. You can also, within your TFSA, invest in Money Market instruments or GICs/CDs, redeemable at maturity, to expand your storehouse of increase.

Beyond these, God has given righteous avenues—biblical strategies that multiply your financial margin while advancing His Kingdom. To embrace His ways is to walk in divine efficiency. You grow in wisdom, testimony, and influence.

WISE STRATEGIES TO INCREASE YOUR FINANCIAL MARGIN:

1. Get Married

If you want to succeed financially, get married. If you want to ruin yourself financially, get divorced. If you want to stunt your growth, stay single. In a book titled; *Money Biblically,* one might not expect a lesson on marriage within a financial discourse, yet here it stands—because marriage is divine economics. Beyond companionship, procreation, and intimacy, marriage carries another divine intent: **prosperity.** God Himself instituted marriage as a covenantal framework for multiplication—spiritually, physically, and financially.

"Two are better than one, because they have a good return for their labor." (Ecclesiastes 4:9, NASB)

The Hebrew rendering of *'good return'* reads:

- *Good* — 'better'

- *Return* — 'wages' or 'pay'

Thus, *'good return'* literally means *better wages* or *more pay*. Two incomes under one roof equal multiplied strength and compounded stability. You are not merely sharing life—you are multiplying capacity.

Considering the financial advantages marriage brings to a couple, understand that there are numerous opportunities accessible simply because the two have become one—even in the financial sense. This unity transcends the mere amalgamation of their financial landscape in budgeting; it extends powerfully into the realm of investing.

Some take this teamwork to an elevated dimension by allowing one spouse's income to cover all bills while the other's is devoted fully to investments. The advantage is glorious—an upgrade of divine order. In this way, the margin within your finances expands, boosting your capacity to accelerate your ascent toward the financial destiny of freedom that God desires for you.

Soon, the money produced from your mutual investment portfolio begins generating passive income, and it is as though a third earner has entered your household, contributing silently yet consistently to your financial ascent. In due time, that passive stream may even replace the need for a job altogether. Such is the power of marriage in finances—a covenantal synergy that multiplies, fortifies, and accelerates destiny.

BUDGET FOR MARRIED PEOPLE

In financial covenant, synergy births surplus. Let us consider the principle mathematically. When two partners marry, considering both earning the same income for the purpose of simplicity in explanation; they effectively double their total household income. Yet, because many expenses overlap—housing, food, utilities, transportation—they can each reduce personal outflows while increasing collective savings.

We therefore reduce 2% from each of the five primary budget categories (Housing, Transportation, Healthcare, Food, Entertainment) and transfer the combined 10% margin into the **Savings and Tithe** category. This expanded category becomes the *seed storehouse*—the sacred allocation for tithing, investing, and future security.

Below is the refined illustration assuming **each partner earns $4,337** monthly (the same base used for the single-person budget)

SIMPLE BUDGET (MARRIED COUPLE)		
Total Combined Income: $8,674		
Category	Percentage	Amount ($)
Savings & Tithe	30%	2,602.20
Housing	33%	2,862.42
Transportation	12%	1,040.88
Healthcare	11%	954.14
Food	10%	867.40
Entertainment	4%	346.96

Breakdown and Benefit: Under the single budget, the *Savings & Tithe* allocation was **$867.40** per person. Together, before margin adjustments, the total would have been **$1,734.8.**However, applying the marriage margin principle (10% reclaimed from shared efficiencies), their joint allocation increases to **$2,602.20.**

This marks an **additional $867.40** gain—divided equally, **$433.70** more per person in the same category. Each now allocates **$1,301.10** instead of $867.40, demonstrating how divine partnership increases both *seed* and *storehouse.*

This is covenantal mathematics—where union yields multiplication. Each partner spends less per category due to shared living costs, yet gains more in their savings and tithe portion—the very ground God uses to multiply wealth. Marriage thus becomes a divine system for financial elevation, designed by God for wisdom, prudence, and mutual benefit.

"Two are better than one, because they have a good return for their labor." (Ecclesiastes 4:9, NASB)

That *'good return'* also mirrors investment principles: the more seed sown *(invested),* the greater the harvest *(returns).* Through marital unity, both can sow more—thus reaping more.

Budgets are divine boundaries that preserve blessing. They reveal what may be safely spent and what must be sown. Through such order, God increases your seed and enlarges your harvest.

"Now He who supplies seed to the sower and bread for food will also supply and increase your store of seed and enlarge the harvest of your righteousness." (2 Corinthians 9:10, NIV)

Therefore, marriage—when governed wisely—accelerates wealth building. It doubles the labour, magnifies the yield, and multiplies the storehouse. If you want to increase financially, align with divine order. **Get married. :')**

2. Build Or Join a Financial Growth Team

You were not designed to prosper in isolation. *"Can two walk together unless they are agreed?"* (Amos 3:3, NKJV). The principle is divine — agreement multiplies strength. As it is written, *"Two are better than one, because they have a good return for their labor."* (Ecclesiastes 4:9). Now imagine not just two, but a team united in purpose, discipline, and vision — a fellowship of financial growth.

A **Financial Growth Team** is a small, covenantal circle of like-minded individuals — friends, family, or trusted peers — who pool resources strategically to create larger investments than they could achieve alone. Through legally binding agreements, members contribute a fixed percentage monthly toward joint ventures such as real estate, money-market instruments, or business equity. Returns are distributed proportionately, transparently, and lawfully. This shared system creates *collective strength, shared accountability,* and *financial resilience* — a fortress against uncertainty and economic storms that could easily overtake a single individual.

Such an alliance cultivates discipline. Each member must intentionally manage spending to ensure their contribution remains consistent, sharpening stewardship and curbing waste. It also activates what is called the *law of social capital* — the God-given ability to multiply wealth through relationships, structure, and shared commitment.

In the world's systems, corporations thrive on this very principle of partnership, equity, and shared risk. The righteous should do no less — only with integrity, wisdom, and purpose. You need not be intimate friends to build wealth together; you need only alignment in *vision, values,* and *discipline.*

As Proverbs reveals, *"Wealth makes many friends"* (Proverbs 19:4, NKJV). While such friendships may be superficial, the spiritually mature understand that financial cooperation, when governed righteously, is not about vanity but vision — not about exploitation, but expansion.

A Financial Growth Team is thus a divine instrument of stewardship. It teaches interdependence, order, and collective advancement. It allows each member to achieve in years what might have taken decades alone.

If two can chase ten thousand, how much more can ten accomplish together? Prosperity accelerates in agreement. Wealth, when united under vision, becomes dominion.

PRIESTLY APPLICATION

Your budget is not a spreadsheet — it is an altar of stewardship. Upon it you lay offerings of obedience, discipline, and foresight. Every tithe, saving, and investment made in faith is a sacred transaction between you and the God of Increase. You are not merely managing money; you are *ministering wealth.* Handle your finances as holy vessels — pure, deliberate, and consecrated unto the Lord.

As a priest of your household, bless your finances, do not merely spend them. Lift your budget before God and decree divine order — that no expense devours what was meant to multiply. Ask the Lord to breathe upon your storehouse seed, for *compound interest is the compounding of your seed.* Let your stewardship be worship and your discipline devotion, for *"He who supplies seed to the sower and bread for food will also supply and increase your store of seed"* (2 Corinthians 9:10).

When your finances follow divine law, Heaven's economy responds. Increase follows order, favor follows obedience, and surplus follows faithfulness. Govern your wealth as priest and king — one who decrees, sows, and reigns — and your life will testify of divine prosperity: from faith to faith, from glory to glory, from increase to dominion.

LESSON 5: TIME IS OF THE ESSENCE: BUILDING LASTING WEALTH

JUDGEMENT

When it comes to wealth building, time is your greatest ally and your most unforgiving adversary. Every day you delay saving, you are not merely postponing your financial growth — you are surrendering time your money could have spent multiplying. Prioritize savings now; each seed sown early compounds into a forest later. Let patience anchor your process, for though the effects of compounding begin slowly, they accelerate with divine rhythm. As the seasons pass, your diligence will bear visible fruit — steady, strong, and multiplying — building wealth that lasts, rewarding both your labor and obedience.

Principle: Time is a divine catalyst for increase. Delay it, and you diminish destiny's reward. The longer it takes you to learn and apply God's financial laws, the further behind you fall in the race toward dominion. True wealth is not built in haste; it is cultivated over time. *"Wealth from get-rich-quick schemes quickly disappears; wealth from hard work grows over time."* (Proverbs 13:11, NLT) Each principle you apply early grants your wealth more time to grow. The sooner you start, the longer the Spirit of Increase can breathe upon your seed.

At its core, *compound interest* is the miracle of money multiplying upon itself — interest earned not only on what you saved, but also on what your savings have already produced. It is the divine law of 'seed multiplying seed.' But this law only favors the diligent who begin early. Time is its catalyst; consistency unleashes it. Use modern tools wisely — *compound interest calculators* — to see how your seed grows across time.

Let your financial goals be S.M.A.R.T: Specific, Measurable, Attainable, Relevant, and Time-bound. Technology is not your master but your servant; let it help you see clearly the power of time in motion. For when diligence meets time under divine law, wealth ceases to be a pursuit — it becomes an inheritance.

EARLY BIRD EXAMPLE

If you began working at 22 and earned **$4,337** monthly, you would build your emergency fund over 3 years and then start investing at 25. Setting aside **$433.70 per month (10% of your salary)** and keeping this amount steady *(without raises or increases for simplicity):* **Investment Period:** 40 years (age 25 to 65) **Monthly Contribution:** $433.70 **Annual Contribution:** $5,204.40 **Estimated Interest Rate:** 5% (compounded annually)

At age 65, your investments would have grown to approximately **\$62 8,690.35**, based on this interest rate and plan. Over the 40 years, you would have contributed a total of **\$208,176**. This calculation assumes the monthly investment does not increase even if your salary rises *(for simplicity)*. To get higher returns, it is wise to raise your investment by at least **10% every time your income increases.**

Because you were content with your *lot in life*, your wealth grew over time. Always have the end in mind from the beginning, for foresight breeds discipline in financial management. Many reach their later years unprepared—forced either to work longer to survive or to become burdens to their families, a state nobody wants to become to their families.

The way to escape this fate is to prepare early. For ease in serving God in the future, master your finances now. Wealth frees the mind to focus on divine purpose; it conquers needs. Understand this—it is not the chasing of money that sustains a man, but the building of wealth that conquers need. This is the only lasting solution. You will thus have a *good journey*, for a journey hampered by lack is not good.

As Solomon said, *"A feast is made for laughter... and money is the answer for everything."* (Ecclesiastes 10:19, NIV). The phrase *"money is the answer for everything"* is a *hyperbole*, an exaggeration to drive home a truth: most of life's challenges can be resolved by financial preparedness.

Money, in proper perspective, is a servant of divine purpose. Understanding its place and power—and knowing that its abundance is built over time—the wise begin early. For those who ignore or mishandle these truths will, in the long run, face unnecessary financial hardship.

TARDY BIRD EXAMPLE

If you start investing at 45 and invest **$1,000 each month: Monthly Investment:** $1,000 **Annual Contribution:** $12,000 **Length of Time:** 20 years (age 45 to 65)**Interest Rate:** 5% (compounded annually)

So; At 65, you'll have **$396,720** after 20 years. **Total Invested:** $1,000 × 12 × 20 = **$240,000**

The Tardy Bird invests **$31,824 more** than the Early Bird (who invested $208,176 total), yet finishes with just **$396,720**, which is about **$231,970 less** than the Early Bird's $628,690.35. Even though the Tardy Bird put in more overall, starting late robbed him of time for increase.

When it comes to building wealth, time is of the essence—small amounts started early can outgrow large amounts started late. The sooner you apply God's principles, the longer your wealth has to grow. The longer you delay, the less time you give your seed to multiply. Wealth grows over time!

The place and importance of money in serving divine purpose is indispensable. Money is a tool of kingdom service, a vessel through which purpose is amplified. Now is the time—build wealth with discipline, with foresight, and with divine intentionality. For the wealth you build today will empower your effectiveness tomorrow as you fulfill your holy assignment upon the earth.

THE SUBSTANCE THAT ATTRACTS INCOME

Principle: Money is drawn to *names with substance*. If there is no weight, excellence, or value attached to your name, money will not stay with you—it will pass you by. Add substance to your name. Education, innovation, intellectual property, business acumen, eloquence, skill, agriculture, creativity, and diversified assets—these are all forms of substance.

The more you cultivate them, the more *magnetic* your name becomes. Suddenly, income begins to locate you. It is as though money now knows both your *name* and your *address.* The heavier your name grows in worth, the more financial inflows gravitate to you—whether directly or passively.

Just as your résumé earns you promotion in your workplace, so too your skill and productivity earn you entrance into higher financial streams. Money has a gatekeeper, and that gatekeeper is man. For man to release resources to you, you must first *offer value.* Without substance, your interactions hold no weight in the realm of exchange.

The goal, therefore, is not to chase money, but to become *weighty*—to add intellectual, creative, and moral gravity to your name until money is compelled to find you. This is **the Law of Substance in Identity**—the principle that your *stature determines your streams.*

Your substance becomes the magnet of your income; it is the force that multiplies your sources of supply. Discover your unique gifts and refine them—your divine endowments are keys to acceleration. They amplify your ability to earn, allowing you to direct the overflow toward building wealth—tithing first, saving second, and investing third. As your substance grows, your financial growth compounds. It is a *holy cheat code* for faster wealth building. Take charge of your uniqueness; it is heaven's currency for dominion in the marketplace.

ANALOGY:

Centuries ago, when ancient communities survived by hunting, they realized how unsustainable it was to keep chasing their prey. Each hunt demanded exhaustion and uncertainty—they never knew where the herds would migrate next. Wisdom was therefore born, and with it, the 'innovation of domestication.' Humanity learned to set bait, attract prey, trap it, retain it, and multiply it. What once required daily pursuit now became a self-sustaining system. Domesticated animals multiplied, producing abundance and security for entire tribes. Hunting became optional—no longer a matter of survival, but of strategy.

INTERPRETATION

In the same way, modern man hunts his prey—*money*. But the wise no longer chase it; they attract and domesticate it. Substance is your bait. Without it, you'll always run after what keeps fleeing. Add value, and money begins to seek you. Once caught, do not squander it. As ancient men preserved and multiplied their herds, so must you preserve and multiply your earnings. Save first—*this is how you retain your prey*. Then invest—*this is how you domesticate it.* Finally, let compound interest make it *multiply* for you, as breeding multiplied the early herds.

Wealth, therefore, is not found in pursuit but in mastery of attraction and management. Your substance is your bait. Your wisdom is your trap. Your investments are your herds. Steward them well, and your barns will overflow by the power of compound interest.

Dangers of Employment as a Primary Financial Safeguard

A job offers a short-term solution to a long-term challenge, and while there is nothing inherently wrong with keeping or seeking employment, the true danger lies in relying on it as your primary source of financial sustenance. Living paycheck to paycheck is not God's design—for it is a manifestation of imprudence. We are called to use the benefits of short-term solutions like employment to build lasting capacity—to construct a system of sustenance, a financial ark, that will keep us afloat in times of inevitable economic storms.

True financial security is forged when we harness employment as a stepping stone, saving for the future and investing wisely. The starkest biblical illustration of the consequences of neglecting this principle is found in the days of Joseph. After seven years of abundance in Egypt, the severe famine hit. In the very first year of famine, all of Egypt came to Joseph asking for food—clear evidence that, despite years of prosperity, the people had saved nothing and lived entirely for the moment. Genesis says, *"When the money of the people of Egypt and Canaan was gone, all Egypt came to Joseph and said, 'Give us food. Why should we die before your eyes? Our money is all gone.'"* (Genesis 47:15, NIV.)

Their imprudence left them dependent, ultimately selling themselves as indentured servants just to survive, while Joseph's foresight and discipline preserved and elevated him. This principle separates the rich from the poor—not by innate capability but by intentional preparation. Poverty often traces its roots to a failure to build financial security when the opportunity is present, whether due to ignorance or negative generational patterns surrounding money.

Employment builds someone else's vision; unless you proactively leverage it, you'll forever be assembling someone else's dreams. Those who designed their own destiny through savings and invested in their vision are the ones able to employ you.

Employment's greatest risk is enabling comfort and complacency, disabling your wealth-building potential if it becomes your only safeguard. When employment is your financial foundation, you stand on shifting sand, and every opportunity or idea dies from lack of capacity. Remember, employment is a platform to earn a salary—not an end in itself. Only when its financial benefits are harnessed through long-term savings is employment truly serving you, enabling you to construct systems that secure your future and freedom.

The church, likewise, must rise to financial stature; influence is built on strength, and without financial power, our ability to impact society for Christ is hampered. Money is one of human society's three foundational pillars—alongside sexuality and religion. Where the church lacks firm financial footing, victories are fleeting.

Just as Joseph did, harness the advantages of the present to build a structure that endures when trouble follows. Your financial ark is for you and for others—including those, like Egypt in famine, who will remain ignorant and need help from both poverty and the word of God. Scripture mandates this: *"Whoever is kind to the poor lends to the LORD, and he will reward them for what they have done."* (Proverbs 19:17, NIV) *"He who gives to the poor will not lack, but he who hides his eyes will have many curses."* (Proverbs 28:27, NKJV)

God blesses those who help the poor, but punishes those who refuse. Therefore, build your ark not only for personal survival but so you may fulfill God's command to rescue others when need arises. This is financial stewardship with eternity in mind.

PRIESTLY APPLICATION

In the priesthood of believers, we are not called to *chase money* but to *build wealth* that serves divine purpose. Wealth is the conqueror of need; money is merely its servant. Handle your finances as sacred vessels—pure, deliberate, consecrated unto the LORD. Your account is your temple treasury; your giving is your incense; your investments are your sacrifices that secure future glory.

Seize every opportunity to learn, build, and invest. Only those who prepare in the right season remain afloat in the floods of uncertainty. *"Those too lazy to plow in the right season will have no food at the harvest."* (Proverbs 20:4, NLT). The best time to begin was yesterday; the next best time is now.

"Wealth is a crown for the wise; the effort of fools yields only foolishness." (Proverbs 14:24, NLT).

Wisdom demands wealth—for it is both crown and covering. The fool lives paycheck to paycheck, never seeking understanding. *"The heart of him who has understanding seeks knowledge, but the mouth of fools feeds on foolishness."* (Proverbs 15:14, NKJV). Do not delay in stewarding your finances. Managing your wealth is not worldly—it is priestly. It is the discipline of kings and priests, ensuring that heaven's resources are multiplied for divine use upon the earth.

LESSON 6:
THE BIBLE AND INVESTING — GOD'S WILL CONCERNING WEALTH-BUILDING

JUDGEMENT

The prudent invest—for this is the divine principle of multiplying wealth over time. Saving alone, without the wisdom of investing and the power of compound interest, is mere hoarding—an act born of fear, not faith. If he who sows sparingly reaps sparingly, then he who never sows will reap nothing at all. It is God's will that you make wealth, for poverty paralyzes your potential to fulfill His purposes on earth. Wealth expands your reach; poverty restricts it. The Lord desires that you prosper, not that you drown in debt—for debt is bondage, but wealth grants dominion. When you learn to master money rather than be mastered by it, you walk in divine liberty. For in abundance lies the freedom to fulfill God's specific call upon your life—a life marked by stewardship, conquest, and divine purpose.

The Parable of the Pounds — Luke 19:11–24, *NKJV*

Now as they heard these things, He spoke another parable, because He was near Jerusalem and because they thought the kingdom of God would appear immediately. Therefore He said: "A certain nobleman went into a far country to receive for himself a kingdom and to return. So he called ten of his servants, delivered to them ten minas, and said to them, 'Do business till I come.' But his citizens hated him, and sent a delegation after him, saying, 'We will not have this man to reign over us.' "And so it was that when he returned, having received the kingdom, he then commanded these servants, to whom he had given the money, to be called to him, that he might know how much every man had gained by trading. Then came the first, saying, 'Master, your mina has earned ten minas.' And he said to him, 'Well done, good servant; because you were faithful in a very little, have authority over ten cities.' And the second came, saying, 'Master, your mina has earned five minas.' Likewise he said to him, 'You also be over five cities.' "Then another came, saying, 'Master, here is your mina, which I have kept put away in a handkerchief. For I feared you, because you are an austere man. You collect what you did not deposit, and reap what you did not sow.' And he said to him, 'Out of your own mouth I will judge you, you wicked servant. You knew that I was an austere man, collecting what I did not deposit and reaping what I did not sow. Why then did you not put my money in the bank, that at my coming I might have collected it with interest?' "And he said to those who stood by, 'Take the mina from him, and give it to him who has ten minas.'

"Occupy until I come." — Luke 19:13, KJV

The command is not passive. It is a divine mandate to *do business*, to trade, to multiply what has been entrusted until the Master returns. The Greek connotation is *"carry on business as usual."* Trading, therefore—even in the stock market—is biblical. The faithful servants traded and gained; the fearful one hoarded and lost. Grace saves, but works determine reward. Every parable of Jesus concealed a spiritual truth; this one unveils the divine principle of stewardship and investment.

Jesus spoke this because His disciples expected an immediate kingdom. He corrected their short-sightedness: *Believe He is coming soon, but live and build as though He tarries.* In teaching stewardship, He used money as an analogy, for *physical riches mirror spiritual riches.* 'If you are unfaithful with unrighteous mammon,' He said, 'who will commit to your trust the true riches?' (Luke 16:11). Thus, faithfulness in financial stewardship reveals readiness for spiritual promotion.

The Structure of the Parable

Ten servants—symbolizing *completion or all*—each received one pound, symbolizing *enough.* The number 10 in Hebrew numerology indicates *completeness* or in other words, *all.* The number 1 in Hebrew numerology means *enough.* Therefore, as taught by the parable, God gives every believer enough to prosper.

The principles remain timeless:

1. Spend less than you earn.

2. Save what you don't spend.

3. Invest what you save. This worked in the ancient world; it works still.

A *pound (minah)* equaled roughly a third of a skilled laborer's annual wage—about $20,000 today. Not extravagant, but enough. The servants fall into three categories:

- **Overachievers** (v.16): 1,000% return.

- **Diligent achievers** (v.18): 500% return.

- **Fearful preservers** (v.20): no loss, but no increase.

The last group represents those who live paycheck to paycheck—bound by fear and ignorance. Ignorance said, "You reap where you did not sow." Yet *investing* is precisely that—profiting through others' labor, letting capital work while you rest. The wise know this truth: *money is meant to serve you, not master you.* Through investment, your servant (money) produces its own offspring—compound interest—multiplying over time.

The foolish servant's cry was envy: "You profit without working." His resentment revealed ignorance of divine law. Wealth is never unjust—it is reward for stewardship. God is not unfair; He is *faithful to His word.* "To everyone who has, more shall be given... but from him who has not, even what he has shall be taken." *(Verse 26)*

Principle: *Ignorance keeps men poor.* Knowledge, discipline, and obedience to divine order create wealth that endures. Investment is not greed—it is governance. Dominion over resources is the Father's will.

CONQUERING DEBT

Once free from debt, your financial vision clears. The fog that once blinded foresight lifts, and peace of mind returns. You can now plan, build, and sow into your financial system for growth—not feed the devourer called debt. Debt is a trap that enslaves foresight and suffocates progress. It blocks saving, stifles investing, and delays wealth-building by chaining you to endless repayments. The residue of bad debt lingers like smoke after fire, staining every future plan.

Be strategic—if you must borrow, let it be calculated and manageable. Borrow for what multiplies, not what diminishes. A small, controlled loan to build credit or fund a proven business is wise stewardship. But overall, the divine decree is clear: *"You shall lend to many nations, but you shall not borrow; and you shall reign over many nations, but they shall not reign over you."* (Deut. 15:6, NKJV). Dominion, not dependence, is your covenant stance in the Kingdom's economy.

If you are in debt, fear not. *"For God has not given us a spirit of fear, but of power and of love and of a sound mind."* (2 Tim. 1:7, NKJV). Peace is your posture, not panic. Seek counsel, create a repayment plan, and discipline yourself toward freedom. Debt is a devourer of both seed and peace—it must be confronted first before true wealth can be established.

Two Proven Strategies for Debt Freedom: The Snowball and the Avalanche

Both methods work—your temperament determines which one fits your journey.

1. The Debt Snowball Method

Start small, build momentum. List your debts from smallest to largest. Pay minimums on all except the smallest; direct every extra dollar toward it. When it's cleared, roll that amount into the next. Each victory fuels your confidence and creates a rhythm of triumph. **Pros:** Quick wins, motivation, psychological strength. **Cons:** May cost slightly more in interest over time. Like a snowball rolling downhill, each cleared debt gathers force—momentum becomes mastery.

2. The Debt Avalanche Method

Start with the highest interest rate first. List debts from highest to lowest interest, pay minimums on the rest, and attack the top one with intensity. Once it's gone, move to the next. This strategy saves money in the long run and shortens the total payoff period. **Pros:** Saves more on interest, faster total elimination. **Cons:** Requires discipline; results take longer to *feel.* The avalanche strikes from above—swift, focused, and cost-efficient. It silences the costly debts first, allowing your wealth to rebuild faster.

Which Path Should You Choose?

Both paths lead to freedom; the key is consistency. Choose one, commit wholly, and advance. The goal is not speed—it is sovereignty. To *get out of debt and stay out.* Only then can you truly build, expand, and govern resources as God intends. Debt-free living is not luxury—it is Kingdom order.

Take heart. Arm yourself with knowledge, strategy, and faith. Whether by the snowball's steady rhythm or the avalanche's forceful strike, rise and reclaim dominion over your finances. Freedom from debt is not just financial—it is spiritual warfare won.

PRIESTLY APPLICATION

God has invested in you — gifts, talents, and divine abilities — the very substance that attracts income. Not all are entrusted equally; as it is written, *"To one he gave five talents, to another two, and to another one, each ac-*

cording to his own ability."(Matthew 25:15, NKJV). Each will give account when the Master returns.

God desires not only that you make Heaven but that you have a *good journey on Earth*. Be diligent. Ignorance itself is not sin — remaining ignorant is.

You were bought with a price; therefore, *"do not become slaves of men."* (1 Corinthians 7:23, NKJV). Break the chains of debt. Work deliberately toward financial liberty. Reduce debt, maximize income retention, and build wealth — for wealth conquers need, breaks bondage, and grants the power of maneuverability in destiny.

Honor God with your tithe. *"Bring all the tithes into the storehouse... and I will rebuke the devourer for your sakes."* (Malachi 3:10–11, NKJV). The tithe is not loss — it is covenant insurance. It secures your financial perimeter from the devourers that consume the harvests of the unfaithful. Many unknowingly invite debt by violating this divine hedge. The tithe is a Kingdom investment in divine financial protection. Mark that well.

"The name of the LORD is a strong fortress; the godly run to Him and are safe. The rich think of their wealth as a strong defense; they imagine it to be a high wall of safety." (Proverbs 18:10–11, NLT). Wealth without divine covering is illusion; strength without obedience is fragile.

Remember, *"Do not store up for yourselves treasures on earth, where moth and rust destroy, and where thieves break in and steal."* (Matthew 6:19, NIV). Inflation, government corruption, and instability can erode earthly riches, but not so the treasures laid up in Heaven. If your treasure is anchored in God, your heart is guarded by contentment; but if your hope is in wealth alone, you stand upon sinking sand.

Therefore, acknowledge the LORD in your finances. Let Him be your fortress, your defender, and your true treasury. Obey His financial laws, pay your tithe, and He will cover your harvests with His faithfulness. For He never loses His power, and His covenant never fails.

LESSON 7: INVESTING WITH FORESIGHT: UNDERSTANDING COMPOUND INTEREST

JUDGEMENT

Goals must be set, and steps taken in deliberate intention. Prudence must be exercised, and stewardship proven. Managing finances and building wealth may feel daunting, yet with knowledge comes not only power but peace of mind. The worst posture is to shrink back—so engage learning, embrace growth, and pray for understanding. "If any of you lacks wisdom, let him ask of God, who gives to all liberally and without reproach." (James 1:5, NKJV) To secure tomorrow, you must first see it. You cannot attain what you have not envisioned. Foresight is the womb of strategy. Set the right goals, and in time your barns will overflow; your labor will bear fruit, and peace will attend your diligence. Work with the end in mind, and you shall surely prosper.

INVESTMENT VEHICLES EXPLAINED

The wise steward diversifies—knowing that each investment has its purpose under heaven. **Bonds** and **Certificates of Deposit** (CDs) or **Guaranteed Investment Certificates** (GICs) are fixed-income instruments; both involve lending in exchange for interest, yet differ in issuer and risk. Bonds are loans to corporations or governments, offering higher returns for higher risk and longer terms. They are tradable and can be sold before maturity. CDs/GICs, however, are time-bound deposits with banks—government-insured, low-risk, and stable, though less profitable. They prioritize safety over growth.

Mutual Funds allow you to pool resources under professional management. These funds invest across stocks, bonds, and other assets—spreading risk while granting access to diversified portfolios. Yet, beware of management fees that quietly erode returns; count the cost before engaging. **ETFs** (Exchange-Traded Funds) mirror this diversity but trade like stocks—liquid, flexible, and cost-efficient. They grant exposure to markets with ease but still carry the rhythm of market risk.

Stocks, or equities, represent ownership. To own stock is to hold a portion of a company's life and potential. With this ownership comes both reward and responsibility—dividends and growth, but also exposure to volatility. There are two forms: *common stock*, granting voting rights and dividends, and *preferred stock*, offering stable dividends but no voice in governance. Over time, stocks have yielded greater returns than most assets, but only for those who walk in patience, not presumption.

PROCRASTINATION: THE ENEMY OF PROGRESS

"You do not know what will happen tomorrow. For what is your life? It is even a vapor that appears for a little time and then vanishes away." (James 4:14, NKJV)

Life is brief. A pilgrim has no time to waste, for divine purpose demands preparation. Wealth, in God's order, is built—not by haste, but by diligence and time. True wealth is not mere possession, but endurance—the ability to sustain your household across generations. *"A good man leaves an inheritance to his children's children."* (Proverbs 13:22, NKJV)

Procrastination is the enemy of destiny. Many delay because they assume they have time, yet wisdom declares: build today for tomorrow's calling. The righteous steward prepares—not out of fear, but foresight. For in foresight lies freedom, and in preparation, dominion.

COMPOUND INTEREST

Often called the eighth wonder of the world, compound interest is the divine mechanism by which time, patience, and wisdom multiply wealth. It is not mere accumulation—it is acceleration. It is interest earned not only on your initial seed but also upon the fruit of prior increase. It is interest upon interest, a force that transforms steady sowing into exponential harvest. "Wealth from get-rich-quick schemes quickly disappears; wealth from hard work grows over time." (Proverbs 13:11, NLT) God's pattern is gradual growth—faithful stewardship over seasons—until your storehouses overflow. Compound interest rewards patience, diligence, and foresight; it is the mathematics of divine timing.

CAPITAL SCALES WELL: As your capital grows, your returns ascend with it. The same percentage yields greater fruit upon larger fields. Invest $100 at 10%, you earn $10; invest $100,000 at the same rate, you gain $10,000. The rate is constant, yet the reward magnifies because the base has expanded. This is the law of scaling—the first harvest is hardest, but once your ground is fertile, increase quickens. Your first $100,000 may take years of endurance; the next comes faster, the next even swifter, until momentum itself becomes your ally. In this, wisdom whispers: *Grow your seed, for growth compounds.* What once took time will, in time, take less.

WHY THE RICH GET RICHER: The wealthy are not those who merely earn more, but those who *endure longer*. They remain steadfast when markets dip, sowing even when others withhold. History shows the market rises more often than it falls, and those who stay invested reap the fruit of compounded recovery. The rich get richer because they understand time is the true multiplier. Begin early, save diligently, invest consistently, and let patience perform her perfect work. For the principle of compounding mirrors the principle of the Kingdom—what begins as a seed becomes a forest. Steward time well, and wealth will answer.

THE TWO CATALYSTS THAT BOOST COMPOUND INTEREST:

1. **Capital**

2. **Time**

CAPITAL — AIMING FOR CRITICAL MASS

Capital is the seed that compound interest multiplies. Without it, there is no soil for growth. Wisdom demands foresight—planning for the days ahead while others drift aimlessly. To build enduring wealth, you must aim for what is called *critical mass*—the financial threshold where your money begins to grow on its own momentum.

In the realm of finance, this threshold sits around **$100,000**. At this point, your investments begin to 'scale'—they start generating returns that grow faster and faster without increasing your effort.

Think of critical mass as an *ark*—a financial vessel that keeps you afloat when economic floods come. Below that threshold, your growth fizzles; above it, it becomes self-sustaining. Stewardship demands setting tangible steps and short-term goals that lead you there.

The mountain may seem vast, but every deposit is a stone laid in your ark's foundation. Over time, as your seed grows, you'll reach the summit of what once seemed unreachable. The goal is not greed—it is dominion, responsibility, and preparedness. The *good man* leaves an inheritance to his children's children *(Proverbs 13:22)*, and that inheritance begins with wisdom, discipline, and foresight.

If you left **$100,000** in a trust for your grandchildren, compounding at a 7% annual return for 45 years, it would grow to **$2,100,245.18**—even without a single additional deposit. That is the silent power of compound interest—the hand of time multiplying faithful stewardship. To reach this place, learn to use the tools already at your disposal.

Many trusted banks offer **wealth management services**, **investment planning**, and **personalized portfolio advice** for clients reaching this $100k threshold. Do not shy away from counsel; *"In the multitude of counselors there is safety."* (Proverbs 11:14, NKJV).

Seek wisdom, learn, and surround yourself with sound advisors who can help structure your investments and ease the mental fatigue that wealth-building can bring. The humble who seek help will find strength, peace, and structure—and their stewardship will steward them into financial freedom.

THREE PATHS TO REACH CRITICAL MASS FASTER

1. Get Creative in Your Savings

Eighty percent of your spending often yields only twenty percent of true value—the *Pareto Principle*. Examine your expenses; trim the waste. Live below your means, not to appear poor, but to build power. If you can afford a $200,000 house, consider one for less—and redirect the margin to investment. Protect the sacred 20% allocated for savings and sowing. It is the bridge to your critical mass. Luxury for clout consumes the very seed of your future. Be prudent, for the wise save for the harvest, but the foolish spend all they have.

2. Increase Your Value to Increase Your Salary

Wealth responds to value. Advance your education, refine your craft, master your industry. Promotions, certifications, and degrees expand your earning potential. Each level of knowledge opens a gate to greater income, enabling you to reach critical mass sooner.

Remember, God delights in your prosperity, for prosperity empowers generosity. *"You will be enriched in every way so that you can always be generous."* (2 Corinthians 9:11, NLT) Elevate your worth—spiritually, intellectually, and professionally—and wealth will be drawn to the excellence you embody.

Even Jesus taught the principle of differentiated value in the Parable of the Workers in the Vineyard (Matthew 20:1–16). In this parable, a landowner went out early in the morning to hire workers for his vineyard, agreeing to pay each of them a denarius—a standard wage for a day's labor.

Those who worked from early morning and those hired later in the day all received the same pay. A denarius, though fair, represented the **common laborer's wage**—the compensation of unskilled field hands waiting in the marketplace to be hired. Historically, this daily wage would equal roughly **$75–$100 today**, the payment customary for lower-ranking laborers who had little education or specialized skill. Such men relied on being hired day to day, with no long-term security. The message is clear: **build your value to expand your earning potential.**

3. Create Passive Income Avenues — Add Substance to Your Name

Your name must become a vessel that produces even when you rest. Build systems, assets, and ventures that earn while you sleep—investments, royalties, rentals, content, intellectual property. When your name has substance, it attracts opportunities and resources. Passive income is the modern translation of ancient wisdom: *"Cast your bread upon the waters, for after many days you will find it again."* (Ecclesiastes 11:1) Let your hands work, but let your seed work harder. This is divine order—your diligence multiplied by time, your wisdom multiplied by capital.

Thus, compound interest is not mere mathematics—it is *God's time-tested law of increase.* Align your stewardship with it, and your wealth will not just grow; it will multiply, preserve, and position you as a vessel of blessing in a shaking world.

PRIESTLY APPLICATION

"Plans go wrong for lack of advice; many advisers bring success." — *Proverbs 15:22 (NLT)*

Surround yourself with wise counsel for financial stability and growth. Fear must never paralyze you from enjoying the fruit of your labor or fulfilling your divine assignments. Meet with trusted financial advisers, understand the risks, and take wise action. Prudence is faith in motion.

Yet above all, trust in Christ. *"I planted, Apollos watered, but God gave the increase."* (1 Corinthians 3:6, NKJV) He alone brings the growth, no matter how skilled your planners or stewards are. Depend on His faithfulness.

Finally, *"Be sure you know the condition of your flocks."* (Proverbs 27:23 NIV) Know the state of your finances. The Church must also care for those who falter in these areas, showing love and provision. Build yourself in wisdom so that your generosity flows from abundance, not lack—giving freely without destabilizing your own house.

LESSON 8: OVERCOMING FINANCIAL FEAR: THE PRINCIPLE OF DIVERSIFICATION

JUDGEMENT

*Money is not evil—it is a tool. It answers many of life's practical needs, offering security, stability, and the ability to fulfill divine purpose. As Solomon said, "The rich think of their wealth as a strong defense; they imagine it to be a high wall of safety." (Proverbs 18:11 NLT). Yet, even those who have prepared well for retirement often battle the fear of losing that sense of security. Beneath their relentless saving and cautious investing lies a quiet adversary—**financial fear**.*

CONQUERING FINANCIAL FEAR: WISDOM FROM SCRIPTURE

"Be sure you know the condition of your flocks, give careful attention to your herds." (Proverbs 27:23 NIV). Your 'flocks' and your 'herds' are your investment assets and general portfolio. They represent your provision and sustainability. Financial fear is conquered through knowledge and stewardship—by maintaining oversight, meeting with financial planners, reviewing your portfolio, and ensuring a healthy balance between risk and return. Information is not just data—it is power, granting confidence and dominion.

"A prudent person foresees danger ahead and takes precautions." (Proverbs 27:12 NLT) Prudence demands preparation. *"Plans go wrong for lack of advice; many counselors bring success."* (Proverbs 15:22 NLT) Wise counsel is the antidote to foolishness. It takes humility to admit what you don't know. Just as you trust doctors with your body and mechanics with your car, entrust your finances to skilled advisers. Surround yourself with an ecosystem of insight—planners, auditors, mentors—each providing clarity to minimize or eliminate unnecessary risks.

THE PRINCIPLE OF DIVERSIFICATION

Developing Your Investment Strategy

Diversification is divine wisdom. It is spreading your resources across various assets, sectors, and regions to reduce vulnerability. *"Send your grain across the seas, and in time, profits will flow back to you. But divide your investments among many places, for you do not know what risks might lie ahead."* (Ecclesiastes 11:2 NLT) This is not fear-based scattering—it is strategy, born of foresight and prudence.

Think of diversification as painting your financial masterpiece—the unique pattern of your 'wealth ark.' Your portfolio should mirror your level of risk comfortability, convictions, and circumstances. *"Be honest in your evaluation of yourselves, measuring yourselves by the faith God has given us."* (Romans 12:3, NLT) Be honest about your tolerance for risk, your emotional responses to volatility, and your stage of life. The young may afford bold strokes of high risk; the mature may prefer steady hues of security. The key is not imitation but authenticity—forge your own path.

Apply the SMART criteria: Specific, Measurable, Achievable, Relevant, and Time-bound goals. Step by step, build toward financial critical mass where compound interest begins to explode for you. Review your goals regularly; they will serve as markers keeping you aligned with your divine trajectory.

COMMON STRATEGIES FOR INVESTING

1. Growth Investing: Focuses on companies poised for rapid expansion. Returns come from capital appreciation rather than dividends. It demands patience and higher risk tolerance but yields significant reward over time. This is the path of visionaries who see beyond the moment. Requires high risk tolerance.

2. Income Investing: Centers on consistent returns—dividends, bonds, or rental income. Lower volatility, steady flow. Ideal for those in retirement or desiring stability. It builds peace and sustains life's steady rhythms.

3. Balanced Strategy: Blends growth and income approaches to harmonize expansion and stability. It spreads risk and balances volatility. This is the strategy of equilibrium—its offers the advantage of a middle path.

There is divine prudence in diversification. The market's uncertainties are many, but wisdom guards the diligent. Be faithful in oversight, humble in counsel, and bold in faith. Fear loses its power where foresight and courage meet.

CHOOSING THE RIGHT STRATEGY

The best investment strategy is the one that aligns with your **financial objectives**, **time horizon**, and **comfort with risk**. Growth investing suits those seeking wealth accumulation and who can endure the market's ebb and flow. Income investing is ideal for those desiring steady cash flow and stability. Balanced strategies attract those who desire a thoughtful blend of both.

Whatever your approach, the pillars remain the same — **consistency, informed decision-making, and alignment with your broader financial plan**. *Be diligent to know the state of your flocks* (Prov. 27:23). Your portfolio is the structure of your wealth-ark. Regular reviews display prudence and faithful stewardship. Occasional rebalancing ensures your investments align with evolving life goals and shifting risk tolerance. As markets fluctuate, rebalancing keeps you anchored, protecting your peace and maintaining equilibrium. Seek professional assistance to avoid costly emotional reactions or misguided decisions.

Stay informed. Understanding the economy, studying market trends, and learning from those more seasoned than you will fortify your discernment. Subscribe to financial news, join investment communities, and lean into wise counsel — *for in the multitude of advisers there is safety* (Prov. 11:14). In finance, knowledge is power; to stay informed is to walk in prudence. Over time, understanding will deepen, confidence will grow, and you will stand firm in mastery.

By developing an investment strategy, you seize the reins of your financial destiny — securing your future by managing your present. You become the architect of a solid foundation that shields your household, funds your pursuits, and empowers your divine mission upon the earth.

REDUCING RISK ACROSS YOUR PORTFOLIO

"Send your grain across the seas, and in time, profits will flow back to you. But divide your investments among many places, for you do not know what risks might lie ahead." (Ecclesiastes 11:1-2 NLT)

The principle of diversification is heaven's antidote to uncertainty. It shields you from market turbulence, providing peace amid volatility. By spreading your resources across different asset classes — stocks, bonds, real estate, and commodities — you build a structure resilient to shifting winds. When one sector falters, another may thrive. Diversification ensures your ark remains buoyant even in stormy financial seas.

Markets are unpredictable. Economic tremors can shake even the strongest sectors, yet a diversified portfolio stands firm — its balance of elements working together to produce growth and stability. Diversification is not fear-based scattering; it is wisdom applied — a shield of foresight around your wealth-ark.

KEY STRATEGIES FOR DIVERSIFICATION

1. Asset Allocation: Spread your investments across various asset classes in proportion to your goals, life stage, and risk tolerance. The mix of stocks, bonds, and other assets should reflect your desired balance between growth and protection. Adjust your allocations as life evolves and markets shift — this is the continual art of financial stewardship.

2. Correlation Management: Know how different investments respond to market conditions. Diversify by combining assets that move differently during economic changes — when stocks decline, bonds may rise or remain stable. This balance cushions your portfolio, ensuring stability through counter-movement. Stocks offer higher growth but greater volatility; bonds bring fixed income and stability. Solid assets like gold serve as steadfast anchors against inflation. Together, they form the framework of your financial resilience.

3. Global Diversification: Expand your portfolio beyond local markets. Investing across nations and regions reduces dependence on any single economy and opens doors to global growth opportunities. This broader reach fortifies your ark against localized storms.

Risk will always exist, but diversification keeps you **afloat amidst financial storms** — steady on course toward destiny. Review your holdings, adjust where necessary, and seek counsel before every major decision. Guard against high investment fees that erode returns; look for cost-effective vehicles like index funds or ETFs for broad market exposure without heavy expenses.

Remain vigilant. Evaluate regularly, stay aware of market movements, and refine your structure as wisdom dictates. Diversification strengthens your ark, stabilizes your emotions, and ensures steady progress even when one stream runs dry. Embrace it — it is the principle of enduring prosperity, a fortress of prudence protecting your God-ordained wealth.

PRIESTLY APPLICATION

"For God has not given us a spirit of fear, but of power and of love and of a sound mind." (2 Timothy 1:7, NKJV)

Fear cripples stewardship. It blinds the believer from divine opportunity and binds the hand meant to multiply. You have not been called to shrink back in timidity but to advance in wisdom, with a sound mind that discerns how to work the principles of increase. Faith must replace fear in your finances; for the same God who grants you seed, grants you grace to multiply it.

If you do not invest, then like the servant in the parable of the pounds who hid his master's money, your portion will diminish in the face of economic shaking. *"For I say to you, that to everyone who has will be given; and from him who does not have, even what he has will be taken away from him."* (Luke 19:26, NKJV) To bury your seed is to betray your purpose. To let fear hinder your release is to forfeit your reward.

Therefore, arise as a faithful steward. Let not fear of loss paralyze your obedience to divine financial principles. Invest, diversify, and build as one who knows his God — for when the floods of crisis come, the wealth of the wise will not drown but rise. In famine, you shall flourish; in downturns, you shall advance. The prudent who walk by revelation shall see increase while others retreat. Let courage, counsel, and conviction govern your hands — for your faithfulness in little shall make you ruler over much.

LESSON 9: BUILDING YOUR FINANCIAL FORTRESS: COVERING YOUR HOUSEHOLD

J UDGEMENT

He who neglects his household has broken divine order. After conquering debt and clearing the path toward freedom, the next move of wisdom is to establish dominion—beginning with stability. Your first fortress stone is the emergency fund; your next, the investment portfolio—your wealth ark. These must then be governed by disciplined flow, through structured household management. The path to financial dominion is simple, but not easy. It demands diligence, prudence, and steadfast obedience. When your emergency fund stands full, and your investments multiply in steady rhythm, it is time to consolidate your household's economy into order—building your fortress and covering your home.

"But if anyone does not provide for his own, and especially for those of his household, he has denied the faith and is worse than an unbeliever." (1 Timothy 5:8, NKJV)

THE THREE PILLARS OF THE FINANCIAL FORTRESS

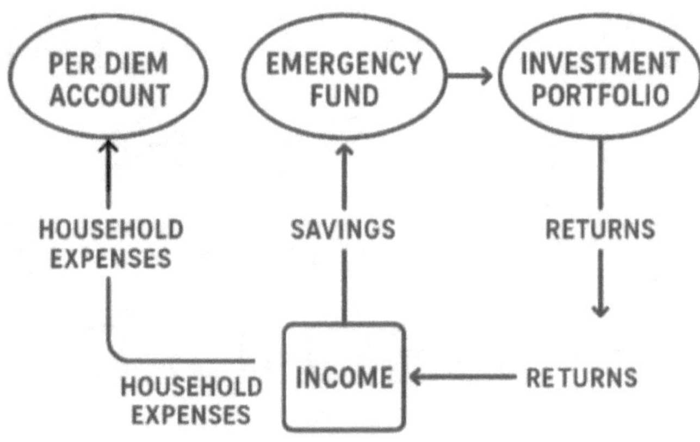

1. The Emergency Fund — Your Shield of Protection

A fortress is only as strong as its foundation, this foundation, and even your first line of defense, is your emergency fund. It stands between you and disaster, shielding you from life's unpredictable blows—job loss, sickness, repairs, or economic shocks. It forms a solid base you can stand on when emergencies come. Without it, a single gust of crisis can bring your house to ruin. With it, you withstand storms and preserve your investments for their purpose—growth.

Start small, but start now. Save your first $1,000, then grow until you have at least three months' worth of living expenses. The diligent increase little by little until the storehouse is full. Keep these funds liquid yet separate, untouched except for true emergencies. This is your shield—your wall of financial defense. Choose the right kind of account to use as your emergency fund; Keep the fund in a high-yield savings account, tax free savings account or money market fund—liquid, but separate from your daily use accounts. The choice is yours.

2. The Investment Channel — Turning Surplus into Soldiers

Once your shield is raised, your army must be deployed. Idle money is wasted potential; it must be set to work. After your emergency fund is full, begin channeling 15–20% of new income into investments—diversified, disciplined, and consistent. Maintain your emergency reserve, but send your surplus into the battlefield of compound interest, where your resources fight for your increase.

Your investments become your soldiers—trained to earn while you sleep, working in fields you do not walk. As your investments mature, returns begin to supplement your income, creating a secondary financial stream. Over time, investment income can help you meet obligations, fund new goals, or further expand your fortress.

3. The PER DIEM System — Governing the Flow

A fortress must have order within its walls. *Per diem* is a Latin term meaning **'by the day'** or **'for each day.'** In personal finance the PER DIEM system is your command center, where discipline governs every day's outflow. It is a consolidation of all household spending into one controlled account, stocked with two months' worth of expenses. Reimburse it each month, and let all payments—fixed and variable—flow through this one channel.

This structure brings simplicity, transparency, and control. It eliminates financial clutter and empowers you to see the true movement of your wealth. You will know the state of your flocks, and every dollar will serve its divine assignment. This is stewardship perfected—governed flow, not emotional drift.

These three—Protection, Growth, and Flow—form the pillars of your financial fortress. With your emergency fund as your shield, your investments as your army, and your PER DIEM as your command post, your household stands fortified, balanced, and blessed. Dominion begins at home. Order produces peace. Peace becomes strength. And strength begets influence.

Faithful stewardship is not reactionary—it is foresighted preparation. The wise foresee trouble and are ready before it comes. Build your fortress now, and you will not fear tomorrow.

The Fortress Framework Summary

Stages 1-3	Purpose	Action
Emergency Fund	Protects against unexpected shocks	Save 3–6 months of essential expenses
Investment Portfolio	Builds wealth through growth	Redirect 15–20% of post-savings income into investments
PER DIEM Account	Maintains daily financial discipline	Manage all expenses through a consolidated operating account

PRIESTLY APPLICATION

A man whose house is not in order cannot lead God's people. Paul taught that the qualifications of leadership begin not in the pulpit but in the home. *"For if a man does not know how to rule his own house, how will he take care of the church of God?"* (1 Timothy 3:5, NKJV) Divine authority begins in domestic order. A disordered household disqualifies divine mandate.

Set your house in order. Build structure, not chaos. Cover your family with provision. The same God who entrusted you with vision requires steward-ship of your household economy. For provision is priesthood—covering those under your care as God covers you. To neglect this is to betray covenant; to uphold it is to walk in divine dominion.

You have not been called to live at the mercy of circumstances but to govern them. Build your fortress—strong, layered, enduring. Let your emergency fund be the wall that shields, your investments the soldiers that conquer, and your PER DIEM system the order that sustains peace. Then your household will not merely survive the storms but stand as a citadel of divine wisdom—an emblem of godly governance and kingdom excellence.

Rule your house well, and your dominion shall expand beyond it. Steward well, and you will be made ruler over much.

LESSON 9 PART B: INSURANCE COVERING AND RISK MANAGEMENT

Faith without works is dead. To trust God is to move responsibly, never presuming on divine protection while neglecting earthly stewardship. For, "You do not know what will happen tomorrow." (James 4:14, NKJV). Faith divorced from prudence is folly, and prudence divorced from faith is idolatry. True balance honors God by using what He provides—insurance among them—to secure not only your life and household but the divine purpose of your wealth. By insuring your assets, you act in 'faith that works,' and the LORD, seeing your diligence, adds His covering—the ultimate assurance.

FORMS OF INSURANCE

Insurance is not about fear but foresight—it preserves peace, stability, and legacy.

Health Insurance: Health insurance serves as your protective shield in a world where medical costs can derail financial plans in a moment. With the right health coverage, emergencies become manageable and your peace of mind flourishes, grounded in foresight and wisdom.

Understand the terms of your policy; deductibles *(the amount you pay before insurance kicks in)*, co-pays *(the fixed fees for the specific service)*, and out-of-pocket limits. Without it, even short-term illness can cause long-term financial loss.

Auto Insurance: A mark of responsible ownership. Liability coverage *(legally required in most regions)*, collision, comprehensive, and uninsured motorist coverage ensure one mishap does not ruin years of effort.

Home Insurance: Safeguards your dwelling and possessions. Renters or owners alike need protection against fire, theft, or disaster. *Homeowners insurance* covers property, possessions, and liability. *Renters insurance* insures personal belongings and liability; structural protection comes from your landlord's policy.

Life Insurance: This is not pessimism but prudence and love made tangible. "Which of you, intending to build a tower, does not first sit down and count the cost?" (Luke 14:28, NKJV). This is being considerate in love. *Term life insurance* offers affordable coverage for set periods. *Whole life insurance* covers you for life and builds cash value, with higher premiums.

The right amount of coverage considers your family's needs, outstanding debts, and future goals—ensuring your loved ones are not left in hardship but have a foundation after your departure.

Liability Insurance: Guards your reputation and resources in a litigious age. It protects you if you're held responsible for injury or property damage to others. Umbrella policies add further protection for those with greater assets to defend.

HOW TO CHOOSE AND MAINTAIN COVERAGE

List your key risks—health, home, income, liability—and review your assets and debts. Select coverage that slightly exceeds your minimum need, guarding against underinsurance. The risk of being under-protected can bring devastation far greater than the expense of an adequate policy. Treat insurance not as an expense but as a covenant of stewardship: a shield that preserves your labor and liberates you to pursue purpose without fear. *"In the multitude of counselors there is safety"* (Proverbs 11:14, NKJV). Seek wise counsel from insurance experts, review policies often, and adjust as life evolves.

Insurance, at its essence, is faith in action—a discipline of foresight that honors God through stewardship. The wise build financial walls before storms arise. Secure now, and heaven's peace will rest upon your prudence.

PRIESTLY APPLICATION

Even if the watchmen stand guard upon the walls, their vigilance is vain if the LORD Himself is not their Keeper. "Unless the LORD watches over the city, the watchmen stand guard in vain." (Psalm 127:1, NIV). This divine principle unveils the hierarchy of protection—man may prepare, but only God preserves. Insurance, investments, and prudent planning are marks of wisdom, yet they remain powerless without the breath of divine oversight. The world may insure possessions, but Heaven insures purpose.

Earthly insurance is not unbelief; it is obedience to the principle of stewardship. It declares that you are mindful of what Heaven entrusted to your care. But wisdom cries louder—true security is not found in policies but in Presence. For while insurance may safeguard your belongings, only the Almighty guards your destiny, your household, and your soul. When the storms rise beyond human comprehension, and clauses fail to cover the calamity, it is the shadow of His wings that becomes your true refuge. "Have mercy on me, O God, have mercy on me, for in You my soul takes refuge. I will take refuge in the shadow of Your wings until the disaster has passed." (Psalm 57:1, NIV).

This is the equilibrium of divine wisdom: the prudent insures his home, but the righteous bows his heart. One drafts his forms in ink; the other inscribes his faith upon the altar. Both are wise—but only the latter is complete. For "The name of the LORD is a strong tower; the righteous run into it and are safe." (Proverbs 18:10, NKJV). The mature believer understands that the fortress of faith and the fence of foresight must stand together. Earthly diligence defends your portion, but divine dependence preserves your inheritance.

"He who dwells in the secret place of the Most High shall abide under the shadow of the Almighty." (Psalm 91:1, NKJV). Here lies the mystery of divine insurance: His angels are your claim adjusters, His promises your coverage, His covenant your policy, His blood your proof of assurance. No disaster, plague, or economic storm can breach the fortress of His faithfulness.

Therefore—guard what the LORD has given you, but never cease trusting the Giver Himself. Build prudently. Secure wisely. Pray fervently. Abide continually. For your earthly insurance may protect your assets, but divine insurance preserves your destiny. In God alone stands the fortress that cannot fall, and under His wings rests the wealth that cannot perish.

LESSON 10:
TAX LIABILITIES:
CAESAR'S PORTION

J UDGEMENT

"Render therefore to Caesar the things that are Caesar's, and to God the things that are God's." (Matthew 22:21, NKJV) *Here lies divine balance—the twofold stewardship of heaven and earth. The tithe is God's holy portion; the tax is Caesar's lawful claim. Both demand faithful observance, each flowing from the same principle of divine order. To honor both is to demonstrate integrity before men and righteousness before God. The one sanctifies your income before Heaven; the other secures your standing within the systems of the earth.*

The faithful steward does not resist taxation, but neither does he bow to ignorance. For while Caesar's percentages may seem unyielding, wisdom provides keys to lighten the burden lawfully. *"My people are destroyed for lack of knowledge,"* (Hosea 4:6, NKJV) — even in matters of finance. Tax deductions, credits, and legal exemptions exist not as loopholes, but as tools of stewardship to preserve the fruit of your labor. The one who neglects to learn them, pays a price not of law, but of laziness.

Thus, as you render to Caesar—*The government*, do so wisely, strategically, and with understanding. To tithe is obedience; to manage tax is stewardship. Both are demanded of the faithful servant—one unto Heaven, the other under Heaven.

TYPES OF INCOME AND THEIR TAX EFFECTS

The wise steward must discern how income is formed and how it is taxed, for ignorance in this area leads to unnecessary loss. The Word teaches, *"Be sure you know the condition of your flocks, give careful attention to your herds."* (Proverbs 27:23, NIV). This includes knowing how every stream of your income is taxed, and how to protect your wealth accordingly.

1. DIRECT (EARNED) INCOME

This is the fruit of your labor—your salary, wages, or self-employment earnings. It is straightforward, familiar, and most heavily taxed. Here, discipline and planning are vital. Keep records and leverage allowable deductions to lessen your liability and increase your savings.

2. PASSIVE INCOME

This is income that continues to flow with minimal effort after initial work or investment—royalties, licensing fees, rental income, or earnings from digital products. It represents the creative extension of your name. While it, too, is taxed, it often allows for deductions related to expenses, depreciation, or management costs. Learn these and apply them—your creativity is a divine resource, but it must be managed with understanding.

3. PORTFOLIO INCOME — YOUR WEALTH-ARK

Portfolio income arises from your investments—dividends, interest, and capital gains. It is where the wise multiply their treasure and where the foolish are devoured by ignorance. Some investments, like ETFs or tax-free accounts, offer legal tax efficiency—allowing growth and even withdrawals free from taxation. Long-term capital gains often carry lower rates than short-term gains; thus, patience itself becomes a wealth strategy. This is wisdom: to let your investments mature like fruit in season, that Caesar's share may lessen while your storehouses increase.

TAX LIABILITY AND MARGINAL TAX RATE

Your **tax liability** is the total amount you owe the government, determined not just by your income, but by how it is structured and declared. As income rises, your **marginal tax rate** determines how each additional dollar is taxed. Understand—moving into a higher bracket does not mean all your income is taxed at that rate, only the portion above the threshold. Many panic at this without knowledge and fall prey to unnecessary fear. Knowledge calms anxiety; stewardship brings mastery.

DEDUCTIONS AND CREDITS: TOOLS OF HOLY SHREWDNESS

"Be wise as serpents and harmless as doves." (Matthew 10:16, NKJV)

Herein lies the holy shrewdness every believer must master. **Deductions** reduce your *taxable income*; **Credits** reduce your *tax owed*. The distinction is crucial.

Deductions: They lower the income upon which taxes are calculated. These may be *standard* (a fixed amount) or *itemized* (specific expenses). Mortgage interest, property taxes, charitable donations, student loan interest, and qualifying medical expenses—each can reduce your taxable income when documented properly. The organized steward reaps where the careless loses.

Keep orderly records; use digital tools or apps to capture receipts and categorize expenses. A prudent system can turn this paperwork into savings come tax time.

Credits: They are even more powerful—they lower your tax *bill* directly. Child tax credits, student loan credits, energy efficiency incentives, or employment-related credits—each directly reduces the amount owed. When properly claimed, they can result in substantial refunds. The righteous must learn the system's language, not to exploit, but to exercise wisdom. For what use is revelation in prayer, if ignorance rules your paper? Heaven rewards diligence in both the spiritual and the practical. :')

STEWARDSHIP THROUGH ORGANIZATION

Order is a mark of divine wisdom. *"Let all things be done decently and in order."* (1 Corinthians 14:40, NKJV)

Whether employed or self-employed, organization is your safeguard. Use technology—tax software, spreadsheets, or apps—to track your earnings and expenses monthly. Keep proof of deductible costs; digitize your receipts. For business owners, freelancers, and the self-employed, timely estimated tax payments prevent penalties that devour profit like locusts. Mark your calendar; let order defend your increase.

Year-round tax planning ensures that Caesar receives only what is his, no more. Regularly review your withholdings, adjust for life changes, and steward your records faithfully. What begins as discipline becomes delight when you see how wisdom preserves your increase.

PRIESTLY APPLICATION

"Everyone must submit himself to the governing authorities, for there is no authority except that which God has established." (Romans 13:1, NIV)

The believer's financial faithfulness extends beyond the sanctuary. To pay your taxes is not bondage—it is obedience. Even Paul admonished, *"Give everyone what you owe him: If you owe taxes, pay taxes; if revenue, then revenue; if respect, then respect; if honor, then honor."* (Romans 13:7, NIV). To pay taxes is to respect divine order in earthly governance. Yet, wisdom demands that you do so shrewdly—paying what is due, but not a penny more than what is owed.

Jesus Himself modeled this balance when He said, *"Render unto Caesar the things that are Caesar's, and to God the things that are God's."* (Matthew 22:21, NKJV). The tithe sanctifies your obedience to Heaven; the tax satisfies your duty to earth. But both require knowledge, discernment, and faithulness. To refuse tax is rebellion; to mismanage tax is folly; to master tax with wisdom is stewardship.

The righteous man does not murmur against taxation but uses the tools of understanding to navigate its systems. He leverages deductions and credits, invests in tax-efficient instruments, and preserves his earnings lawfully. This is not cunning—it is *holy prudence.* For as Joseph stored grain during years of plenty, so too must the believer manage Caesar's portion with foresight.

Therefore, submit with wisdom. Obey with insight. Render to Caesar with precision, and to God with reverence. For while the government's portion secures your peace with the state, God's portion secures your favor in Heaven. Together, they form the full circle of stewardship—obedience on earth, blessing from above.

Let your tax payment be an act of discipline, not despair. Let your diligence in record-keeping be your defense. And let your understanding of law become a weapon of stewardship, ensuring that no unnecessary portion of your harvest is devoured. For this too is dominion—ruling your finances under divine order and earthly law alike.

"Diligent hands will rule, but laziness ends in slave labor." (Proverbs 12:24, NIV). Therefore, steward with wisdom, pay with integrity, and rise with favor—For even Caesar must acknowledge the excellence of a faithful servant of the Most High.

LESSON 11: SECURING THE FUTURE: INVESTING WHAT YOU'VE SAVED FOR RETIREMENT

J UDGEMENT

Starting your retirement planning early is among the most prudent and powerful financial decisions one can make. It is foresight in motion—an act of divine stewardship and matured wisdom. To plan for tomorrow while strength remains today is to walk in the likeness of God, who declares "the end from the beginning" (Isaiah 46:10, NIV). Such planning births peace of mind, for the future no longer lurks as an uncertainty but stands prepared. It unveils strategies to grow your savings, preserve your wealth, and sustain your dignity in the golden years ahead.

Time, when partnered with discipline, becomes a covenant ally. Through consistency, compound interest, and faithfulness, time multiplies quietly. You were not created to endure your latter years in lack but to enjoy the fruit of wise labor—a season of rest, peace, and generational blessing.

Just as God prepares the end from the beginning, you too must plan the sunset of your working years while standing in your morning.

Knowing and Preparing for the End, From the Beginning

A budget is not mere arithmetic—it is revelation. It tells you not only what you can afford to spend, but what you must save to remain secure. It exposes your **'retirement number'**—the total amount you will require to maintain your current standard of living once the paychecks cease.

The Goal: To sustain your lifestyle without dependence on labor. The deception of time makes men delay, but wisdom counts the years while strength still abides. Know what you'll need and begin.

Three Things you Must Know to Calculate Your Retirement Number

1. Your Expenses: Your current expenses mirror your future needs.

- *Bottom-Up Approach:* List every line of expense—housing, food, transportation, health, leisure. Multiply your monthly total by twelve for your annual number.

- *Top-Down Approach:* Begin with your after-tax income, adjust for any new costs or freedoms retirement may bring.

Remember: It is best to **enter retirement debt-free** to remove unnecessary financial weight and bondage to creditors.

2. Your Fixed Income: These are the sure streams: pensions, annuities, and government benefits. Knowing this figure reveals what portion of your needs is already covered before you draw from your savings.

3. The Gap: The gap is the difference between what you'll need and what you'll receive. It is the space your retirement savings must fill—wisely and sustainably.

The 4% Rule — The Safeguard of Sustainability

This trusted rule states that you may safely withdraw **4%** of your total retirement savings in the first year, adjusting annually for inflation, without outliving your resources.

Example: Annual expenses: $60,000 Fixed income: $38,592 Gap: $21,408 *(Annual expenses less Fixed income)* $21,408 ÷ 0.04 = $523,200

Thus, you'll require approximately **$523,200** invested to sustain withdrawals of $21,408 yearly without depletion.

Key Considerations With Financial Advice:

- Diversify between conservative and growth assets to guard against volatility.

- Recalculate at key milestones—ages 40, 50, and 60—as seasons and incomes shift.

- Guard against the *sequence of returns risk*: the danger of poor early returns eroding your savings. Seek counsel.

Age-Based Milestones

At 40: You've likely stabilized your career and family structure. Assess your savings progress and retirement contributions, then adjust accordingly.

At 50: You're near your peak earning potential. Begin taking advantage of *catch-up contributions* in your retirement accounts to maximize tax-advantaged savings.

At 60: These final years are crucial. You're shifting from accumulation to preservation. This is when compound interest takes its strongest effect and when you clarify retirement costs and pay off large obligations.

Wealth With Purpose

"Children should not have to save up for their parents, but parents for their children." — 2 Corinthians 12:14 (NIV). God's order for wealth is generational. Saving and investing are not ends in themselves—they are ministries of foresight. Through disciplined saving and measured withdrawals, your resources outlive you, blessing descendants and advancing divine causes.

"Where there is no counsel is, the people fall; but in the multitude of counselors there is safety." — Proverbs 11:14, NKJV. Seek godly and professional counsel. A certified planner is not a substitute for faith, but a tool of wisdom under it.

Retirement planning is not merely about sustaining income—it is about sustaining assignment. It transforms years of toil into a season of fruitful rest, generosity, and peace. Begin early. Plan faithfully. Steward with reverence.

And when your latter years comes, you will not beg for bread—you will bless many, having prepared, as God Himself does, the end from the beginning.

UNDERSTANDING AND MANAGING RETIRE-MENT RISKS

Once you retire, two unseen forces threaten the longevity of your financial fortress: **the Sequence of Return Risk** and **the Inflation Risk**. Both work subtly, eroding the fruit of decades of labor if left unguarded. Wisdom, therefore, demands foresight and counsel—before and during retirement.

1. Sequence of Return Risk — The Timing Trap

Definition: This risk arises when poor market returns occur early in retirement, precisely when you begin withdrawing from your portfolio. The result is a 'double impact'—your investments shrink while you draw from them, leaving less capital to recover when markets rebound.

Two retirees may start with identical savings and identical average returns—yet if one retires in a market downturn while the other in a boom, their outcomes diverge drastically. Timing, not talent, becomes the divider between sufficiency and scarcity.

Protection Strategies: A wise steward fortifies against this by seeking counsel to make informed decisions. Certified financial planners help mitigate this risk through strategies like:

- **Bucket Strategy:** Dividing your portfolio into short-, medium-, and long-term buckets. The short-term bucket (cash and bonds) covers several years of income needs, shielding your long-term investments (stocks and higher-growth assets) from forced withdrawals during downturns.

- **Dynamic Withdrawal Strategies:** Adjusting withdrawal rates yearly based on performance and market conditions rather than fixed withdrawals.

- **Diversification:** Combining income-generating assets with growth investments to balance stability and opportunity.

Expert guidance here is essential—because once you begin withdrawing, consistent structure becomes your lifeline.

2. Inflation Risk — The Silent Erosion

The second enemy is **inflation**, the slow and steady rise of costs that weakens your purchasing power. It does not roar like recession—it whispers, and over time, it consumes.

The Rule of 72 helps us discern its changes:

- Divide **72** by your expected return to find how many years it takes your money—or costs—to double. At **10%**, money doubles in **7.2 years**. At **3% inflation**, prices double in **24 years**. Thus, today's $60,000 lifestyle will require $120,000 in 24 years—and if inflation rises to **5%**, only **14 years**.

"A prudent person foresees danger ahead and takes precautions. The simpleton goes blindly on and suffers the consequences." — Proverbs 27:12 (NLT)

Nominal vs. Real Returns: Your nominal return is what you see; your real return is what you keep after inflation.

If your investment grows at 3% and inflation is 3%, your true gain is **zero**—your money grew, but your power to purchase did not. Aim not just to grow wealth, but to preserve *its worth*.

Building an Inflation-Resilient Portfolio

Retirement wealth must not only endure—it must expand in *real* value. Bonds, CDs, and high-yield accounts provide stability, but may lose ground over time. A balanced portfolio—anchored in dividend-paying and growth stocks—tends to thrive above inflation's tide.

Many fear the market's volatility, yet when guided properly, *the greater risk is not fluctuation—it is stagnation.* Stocks, wisely chosen and diversified, can protect the purchasing power of your savings far better than conservative accounts that merely tread water.

Thus, as you prepare, remember: volatility is temporary; inflation is perpetual. The wise build not just to survive but to sustain.

Work alongside godly and professional counsel to:

- Structure your portfolio to weather both cycles and storms.

- Adjust withdrawals safely under the 4% rule.

- Ensure your resources *grow in real value* while serving divine purpose.

Retirement must not be a season of fear but of faith-filled wisdom. Build your ark before the flood, scale it with knowledge, and steer it with counsel. For when the economic waters rise, your house shall stand firm—rooted in foresight, girded by wisdom, and upheld by the God who multiplies what is managed well.

PRIESTLY APPLICATION

Your path to a secure and fruitful retirement need not be lonely or fearful. Surround yourself with wisdom—books, trusted advisors, mentors, and those who have walked the path before you. Proverbs 19:20 exhorts, *"Get all the advice and instruction you can, so you will be wise the rest of your life." (NLT).* The wise do not isolate themselves in uncertainty; they gather understanding as a shield for the future.

Scripture declares, *"To acquire wisdom is to love yourself; people who cherish understanding will prosper"* (Proverbs 19:8, NLT). True prudence is an act of self-love, for wisdom protects, prospers, and prepares. The wealth of the wise is not mere luxury but a *crown* and *security* (Proverbs 14:24). Those who seek knowledge early secure peace later. In contrast, *"the heart of him who has understanding seeks knowledge, but the mouth of fools feeds on foolishness"* (Proverbs 15:14, NKJV).

Wisdom demands wealth—not for vanity, but for stability and steward-ship. It is foolish to drift paycheck to paycheck; this is slavery to ignorance. Wisdom calls for diligence, learning, and foresight. Therefore, remain steadfast now, learn continually, and plan wisely; your golden years will not be burdened with anxiety but crowned with abundance. *Be prudent, and your latter end shall greatly increase.*

LESSON 12: HOW THE CHURCH MUST HANDLE ITS FINANCES

JUDGEMENT

If the Church fails in financial integrity, it tarnishes the righteousness it proclaims and weakens its witness before the world. The treasury of God's house is sacred, meant to fund the gospel, not feed greed. When 'Judases' are allowed to handle holy funds unchecked, corruption seeps in, and credibility dies. Holiness too demands oversight. The Church must therefore mirror Heaven's order: transparent, accountable, and free from manipulation. Every coin must be counted with integrity, for stewardship itself is worship. When the Church handles money faithfully, it strengthens its voice and expands its reach—but when it fails, it gives the enemy cause to blaspheme. The purity of the Church is tested not only in its doctrine, but in its dealings.

Jesus Anointed at Bethany

Six days before the Passover celebration began, Jesus arrived in Bethany, the home of Lazarus—the man he had raised from the dead. A dinner was prepared in Jesus' honor. Martha served, and Lazarus was among those who ate with him. Then Mary took a twelve-ounce jar of expensive perfume made from essence of nard, and she anointed Jesus' feet with it, wiping his feet with her hair. The house was filled with the fragrance.

But Judas Iscariot, the disciple who would soon betray him, said, "That perfume was worth a year's wages. It should have been sold and the money given to the poor." Not that he cared for the poor—he was a thief, and since he was in charge of the disciples' money, he often stole some for himself. (John 12:1–6, NLT)

INTERPRETATION

The scene unfolds with Mary pouring costly perfume upon the feet of Jesus—a pure act of devotion. Yet Judas, the keeper of the ministry's money, protests in false righteousness, cloaking greed beneath concern for the poor. The Scripture unveils a painful truth: *he was a thief*, helping himself to what was meant for the work of God.

Herein lies the divine warning—corruption can creep even into holy work when money is mishandled and oversight neglected. The Son of God entrusted finances to others but never managed them Himself, teaching us a vital principle: spiritual leaders must oversee vision, not vaults. To merge the pulpit with the purse is to invite temptation and blur the sacred with the secular.

Therefore, every church must establish **a system of divine order** in its financial affairs—transparent, accountable, and fortified. Every coin counted. Every gift documented. Every hand that touches money observed by another. This is not distrust—it is discipline. Ezra's leadership modeled this when he recorded every ounce of silver, every vessel of gold, every gift of value with unwavering precision (Ezra 8:33–34).

A church without financial structure becomes a marketplace; and a pulpit without oversight, a snare. Remember how Christ, in righteous anger, drove out the money changers (John 2:13–16). He restored reverence to His Father's house, declaring, *"My house shall be called a house of prayer."* The modern church must do no less. Its funds must serve the gospel, not greed.

Thus:

- **A professional accounting system** must be in place.

- **A finance committee** must regularly conduct audits.

- **Clear Checks and balances** must ensure no single person controls money alone.

- **Elders** must approve expenditures without directly handling cash.

Such discipline protects both shepherd and sheep. It builds trust, fosters transparency, and declares to heaven and earth that this ministry is above reproach.

A church that honors these principles becomes a fortress of integrity. Its wealth flows not from manipulation but from obedience. For when the

LORD says, *"Bring all the tithes into the storehouse"* (Malachi 3:10, NKJV), He is not calling for greed but for governance—to ensure that His house is ever supplied, His people ever sustained, and His mission ever advancing.

The Church must never beg, for begging is beneath a covenant people. Provision flows through obedience. *Tithes* and *offerings* are the ordained channels of sustenance; merchandise and fundraising should be sold **at cost or less**, ensuring fundraising or promotional efforts are not for profit and do not dilute tithes and offerings, which must be reserved for **building the Kingdom**. Donations given online or otherwise belong to the church, not individuals. To mishandle it is to mock the Giver.

When stewardship aligns with Scripture, surplus is inevitable. For the righteous will never be forsaken, nor their children left begging bread *(Psalm 37:25).*

PRIESTLY APPLICATION

Wisdom is not proven in words—it is proven in results *(Luke 7:35)*. And nowhere is this more evident than in the stewardship of God's resources. To manage divine provision faithfully is to mirror the wisdom of Heaven on earth. Every coin in the treasury is a test of trust.

The faithful steward understands that handling the resources of the Kingdom is not a privilege of power but a proof of integrity. To squander the LORD's money is to despise His trust; to multiply it is to honor His grace. Therefore, let every minister, treasurer, and trustee remember: they are not owners but keepers of what belongs to God.

Build the church's financial house with order, foresight, and reverence. Record every transaction. Guard against secrecy. Employ professionals.

Audit continually. And above all, pray before you spend. This is how wisdom manifests—by merging spiritual discernment with practical diligence.

Let no man in ministry confuse generosity with recklessness, nor frugality with faithlessness. The balance is stewardship: guided by Scripture, managed by systems, sanctified by prayer. When the Church governs its resources with righteousness, God entrusts it with abundance.

The proof of wisdom is fruit. The fruit of financial wisdom is sustainability. And the fruit of sustainability is Kingdom advancement. Thus, let the Church of Christ rise in order, integrity, and surplus—rich in resources, richer in righteousness.

For the LORD of the harvest supplies seed to the sower, not to the squanderer. Let the modern Church therefore sow with precision, reap with joy, and account with holiness—that Heaven may say once more, *"Well done, good and faithful steward."* (Matthew 25:23, NKJV)

LESSON 13: FORGING YOUR FINANCIAL PLAN

JUDGEMENT

Having gathered every principle taught herein—the art of sowing, the stewardship of saving, and the prudence of investing—the time has come to act. Tools unused rust in the shed; wisdom unpracticed decays into regret. Therefore, set your hand to the plow—build, plan, and pave your road to enduring wealth. "Commit your works to the LORD, and your thoughts will be established" (Proverbs 16:3, NKJV). Financial dominion is not attained by prayer alone but by prayer-infused discipline, faith-inspired structure, and the Spirit's guidance in execution. A plan forged in divine counsel endures the tempests of uncertainty, for it is anchored in eternal principles, not fleeting trends.

THE STRUCTURE OF FINANCIAL STEWARDSHIP

Your financial statements are not mere papers—they are the mirrors of your stewardship. They tell the truth about your diligence, foresight, and discipline. *(Proverbs 27:23).*

The **budget** is your guardrail—it keeps your spending aligned with your purpose. Within it, your **Tithe** and **Savings** stand as sacred 'no-touch' categories, reserved for covenant and security. Every other allocation—such as per diem, investment, insurance, and giving—is adjustable but must remain disciplined.

Your **income statement** follows, revealing how faithfully you have walked within your budget. Then comes your **balance sheet**, laying bare your assets, liabilities, and true *net worth*—the state of your household under Heaven's watch.

True wealth is not measured by your balance but by your ability to sustain your life's purpose without fear or toil. Financial literacy is not secular knowledge—it is spiritual maturity in motion. To neglect planning is to despise wisdom; to waste increase is to dishonor the Giver. The *fool* consumes without thought; the *wise* multiplies through foresight.

Your **cash flow statement** is the final revelation—it shows your surplus, your margin, your breathing room. That surplus is your seed; reinvest it. Let no idle money dwell long in your accounts—money must move, or it dies. As Isaac sowed in famine and reaped a hundredfold, so must you invest in seasons when others retreat.

The markets may shake, but the hand of a faithful steward never trembles, for faith is the anchor beneath his ventures. Build your financial structure as a living covenant. Review and revise often. Seek counsel, read, learn, and grow. Celebrate each milestone, for the LORD rejoices in humble beginnings.

Wealth without purpose is vanity; wealth with divine intent is ministry. As you prosper, remember: the purpose of wealth is not indulgence but impact. Let your increase fund Kingdom work, uplift others, and broadcast the generosity of Christ through your stewardship. For money in the hands of the righteous becomes a message—one that preaches louder than words.

KNOWLEDGE TO FORGE YOUR PLAN: A BRIEF GLOSSARY

- **Compound Interest**: Refers to Interest that earns on both the principal and accumulated interest. Begins small, but over time, multiplies like seed sown in fertile soil. It is the divine principle of multiplication mirrored in finance.

- **Dormant Asset–Active Liability (DA.AL)**: Assets that drain instead of grow; an asset due to value but draining cash flow through costs. Examples are homes or vehicles that consume but don't produce. Identify and manage them wisely. Recognizing DA.ALs separates true builders from consumers.

- **Investments Portfolio:** This is your **wealth-ark**—the structured landscape showing how your investments are spread across different assets, applying the principle of **diversification** to reduce risk and increase growth stability.

- **Portfolio Diversification**: The practice of spreading investments across various assets to reduce exposure to loss—wisdom's way of guarding against uncertainty.

- **Withholdings**: Tax amounts deducted at the source (pay-as-you-earn), ensuring obligations are met continuously rather than in one sum; manage your income and tax bills with this in mind.

PRIESTLY APPLICATION: THE THREE PILLARS OF FAITHFUL STEWARDSHIP

Commitment. Accountability. Responsibility. These three pillars uphold every lasting work under Heaven. Commitment anchors your word with action. Accountability is the mirror of your progress; it humbles you, aligns you, and preserves you from deviation. Responsibility is the discipline of stewardship—your acknowledgment that what you hold is not your own, but God's, entrusted for a time and purpose.

A prudent steward lives by these three: committed to purpose, accountable to wisdom, and responsible before God and man. Together, they form the architecture of faithful prosperity. Wealth built on these pillars stands unshaken when the rains descend and the floods rise.

Let your financial plan be tempered by wisdom, sealed in prayer, and executed in excellence. Then shall you stand when others fall, for your foundation is laid upon the Rock, not the sand of impulse and presumption.

If these principles be kept, you shall rise above the storm, prosper in the famine, and rule amidst the ruins. If neglected—

'après moi, le deluge!'

'après moi, le deluge!'

MONEY BIBLICALLY

CLARION CALL

To steward your finances well is to love well—love in action, not in words alone. It is love toward your household and dependents, and love toward God, for managing what He entrusts honours His Lordship *(James 2:17)*. God so loved the world that He gave—He acted. His love was proven in His giving. In that divine act, He offered His Son, Jesus Christ, who died and rose again, granting us eternal hope and Salvation.

Though to learn about money is wisdom, for wisdom is much better when you have money, for with it you have the power to put some of your wisdom to effect. The Bible teaches that only wisdom, not money, can save your life. *(Ecclesiastes 7:11-12)*. And what wisdom is this? The wisdom to choose eternal life in Christ Jesus. As Deuteronomy 30:19 commands, *"I have set before you life and death, blessing and cursing; therefore, choose life, that both you and your descendants may live."* (NKJV), and with wisdom, you make the right choice.

Yet what will it profit a man if he gains the world but loses his soul? (Mark 8:36). Earthly wealth fades—its glitter deceives, its promise wanes. *"Riches won't help on the day of judgment, but right living is a safeguard against death"* (Proverbs 11:4 NLT). Build wisely, with eternity in view. *"Trust in*

your money and down you go! But the godly flourish like leaves in spring"
(Proverbs 11:28 NLT).

Let your wealth serve eternal purpose—giving, loving, serving God with a pure heart. For if you possess riches yet have not love, you have nothing *(1 Corinthians 13)*. God is love; without Him, wealth is hollow. Money is a pilgrim's tool—it builds bridges of impact but cannot buy eternity. Tragic is the soul who gains the world's treasures yet hears, 'Depart from Me.' But there is hope—for Christ is the Way, the Truth, and the Life; no one comes to the Father except through Him *(John 14:6)*.

To surrender to Him is to secure your soul. Yield to Him, and His love, guidance, and Spirit will lift you above the floods of uncertainty and pain, anchoring you in peace and purpose in this world and beyond.

Prayer of Surrender

"Dear God, Heavenly Father of all who trust in Your Son Christ Jesus, hear my prayer. I yield my all to You—I give You me, all of me. Take this life and mold it into Your enduring essence. I believe Christ died in my stead as sacrifice for my sins and rose again for my justification. By trusting in Him, I am saved from eternal condemnation. I believe with my heart and confess with my mouth, and thus I am Yours. I am Born Again. AMEN."

And now, with the gift of salvation, you have access to ask anything in the name of Jesus Christ, and it shall be granted unto you.

Prayer of Launching

Dear Holy Spirit, I acknowledge that this journey of financial literacy and management is not a one-time event but a lifelong path—of learning and unlearning, shifting and adapting, remaining steadfast and afloat. I ask that You grant me the power to make wealth, as Your Word promises, O God. Help me build a wealth ark that shields not only me and my household, but one that grants abundance and surplus, that I may be a blessing in this world and wield the influence needed to win souls for the Kingdom of God.

Give me the right heart concerning matters of money—that I may not be corrupted by its accumulation, that the love of it may not be found in me, but that I may remain a pure steward of all You entrust to my hands, managing it for Your glory alone. Grant me the grace of purity and wisdom abounding. Bestow upon me the shrewdness I require, the knowledge, the understanding, the prudence and discretion, the diligence and discipline necessary for this sacred stewardship. I ask all this in the mighty and glorious name of Jesus Christ. AMEN.

And now—

"The LORD bless you and keep you; The LORD make His face shine upon you, and be gracious to you; The LORD lift up His countenance upon you, and give you peace." *(Numbers 6:24–26, NKJV)*

Excel in your wealth-building. Steward your finances with righteousness. For soon the King shall stretch forth His hand and say—"Well done, good and faithful servant... Enter into the joy of your Lord."*(Matthew 25:23, NKJV)*

SHALOM and MARANATHA.

CHRIST'S Faithful Vassal,

JEHU :')

About the author

Yeshua S. Jehu, authors the five-book *Shepherd's Pouch* series. Tailored for believers, it tackles power, financial stewardship, wealth-building, destiny fulfillment, spiritual development, and sexual purity—equipping you to stand strong in integrity, mature in truth for leadership, discipleship, relationships, and personal life.

Money Biblically, the second installment of the series, unveils the practical side of wealth-building and financial stewardship through clear, accessible financial literacy education. It introduces unique original concepts that create an atmosphere for deeper understanding, opening readers' eyes to powerful strategies for building wealth faster and more wisely over time.

Interconnected yet standalone, each volume ensures you grow fully equipped, lacking nothing.

Connect with the Author

Follow me on social media to stay updated:
Twitter/X: @Yeshua_S_Jehu
Instagram: @Yeshua_S_Jehu

LinkedIn: @Yeshua Jehu

Stay connected—discover new updates, behind-the-scenes stories, and keep the conversation going. Connect, share, and be part of the journey.

The Shepherd's Pouch: A Five-Book Vision for Biblical Dominion

The Shepherd's Pouch is the visionary name of this transformative five-book series, with *Money Biblically* serving as the powerful second installment. This book equips you with righteous wisdom to master wealth—but it reveals only one of society's three foundational pillars of power.

That profound revelation awaits in *Books 3-5* that follow *Money Biblically*, each delivered with the same consistent excellence—interconnected as a cohesive series, yet individually complete, satisfying, and independent.

Book 1 opened the door to how to manage influence and power with purity and divine cunning. Money Biblically unlocks the first pillar: Finances/Wealth.

These are the three pillars of human society from which dominion over the earth becomes possible through God's divinely set principles—pillars upon which this entire series teaches passionately: **Sexuality, Religion/Spirituality,** and **Finances/Wealth.**

These are the roots of dominion, power, and influence, without which the church cannot wield transformative power for divine effect. Discover how these pillars are rooted in Scripture, first revealed in Genesis 1:28 as the eternal formula for power, as you journey through the entirety of this series.

Experience the *"fruitfulness"* of true spiritual life that pleases God and re-shapes society; the divine *"multiplication"* born from the purity of sexuality, radiating righteous integrity across every avenue of life; the knowledge to build wealth that empowers you to *"subdue"* the earth and enact physical change with authority; and finally, the *"dominion"* that manifests as you master these three pillars through the wisdom and revelation of the Holy Spirit—applied with unshakable practicality.

"Then God blessed them, and God said to them, 'Be fruitful and multiply; fill the earth and subdue it; have dominion over the fish of the sea, over the birds of the air, and over every living thing that moves on the earth.'" (Genesis 1:28, NKJV)

Unlock the complete series and step into your divine authority. God bless you!

Also by Yeshua S. Jehu

THE SHEPHERD'S POUCH Series

Book 1: The 48 Laws of Power Biblically

Book 2: Money Biblically

Book 3: The Principle of Becoming

Book 4: The Five Guardians of Spiritual Fervour

Book 5: Purity Rises from Above

"Dare to complete the pouch? Interlock power, influence, purity, and spiritual vitality—unlock their divine interconnectivity. *Hope to see you in the next volume, fully armed."* :')